CAMBRID
Ghosts &

For Chris and Gloria Everett, with love

CAMBRIDGESHIRE
Ghosts & Legends

Polly Howat

COUNTRYSIDE BOOKS
NEWBURY, BERKSHIRE

First published 1998
(Polly Howat 1998

COUNTRYSIDE BOOKS
3 Catherine Road
Newbury, Berkshire

ISBN 1 85306 393 2

Designed by Mon Mohan
Cover illustration by Colin Doggett
Map by Trevor Yorke

Produced through MRM Associates Ltd., Reading
Typeset by Acorn Bookwork, Salisbury
Printed by J.W. Arrowsmith Ltd., Bristol

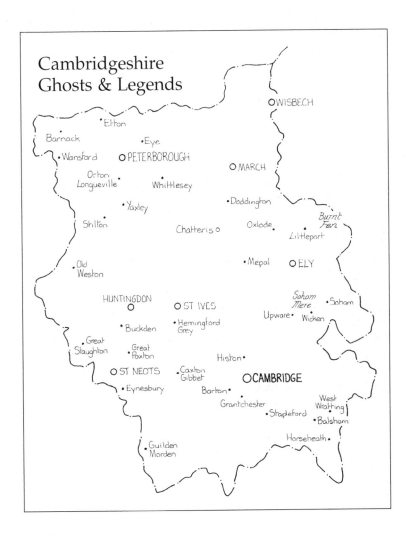

Cambridgeshire
Ghosts & Legends

O WISBECH

• Elton

Barnack

• Eye

• Wansford   O PETERBOROUGH

O MARCH

Orton
Longueville •

• Whittlesey

• Doddington

• Yaxley

Chatteris O

Oxlode •

Burnt Fen

Shilton

• Littleport

• Old
Weston

• Mepal   O ELY

HUNTINGDON
O

O ST IVES

Soham Mere • Soham

Upware •   • Wicken

• Buckden

• Hemingford
Grey

• Great
Staughton

• Great
Paxton

Histon •

O ST NEOTS

• Caxton
Gibbet

O CAMBRIDGE

• Eynesbury

Barton •

West
Wratting

Grantchester

• Stapleford

• Balsham

Horseheath •

• Guilden
Morden

Introduction

Following boundary changes Cambridgeshire today includes the old Isle of Ely, Huntingdonshire and the Soke of Peterborough. It is a region of great variety and contradiction, from vast open levels to gently rolling hills. Sallow gault brickwork is shamed by mellow Barnack stone, old fashioned market towns compete with large modern conurbations, stunningly beautiful religious and college architecture raises the spirits, whilst straight man-made waterways vie with meandering rivers. There are still people who have never been to London living alongside those who have travelled around the world and back again. I have lived in the northern Fens for the last 23 years and love the place.

A great store of folklore and legend is contained within the shire's boundaries. My sources include published works, typewritten manuscripts and handwritten notes jotted down on scraps of paper or carefully recorded in exercise books left half forgotten in cluttered drawers. Equally important is the information gathered from minds and mouths. Traditions and stories were, and to a degree still are, passed from generation to generation, although the art and inclination has declined with the impact of modern technology and resources. Thankfully there are still those prepared to share the old wisdom with 'strangers' over a pint of beer or a cup of tea, which given the time is my preferred method of working.

This is not a dead subject, even though ghosts abound! Some of the following stories and legends will be familiar, for others it is their first time in print. During my research, folklore in the making is often uncovered which I endeavour here to share with the present and preserve for the future.

Polly Howat
Gorefield, Wisbech

BALSHAM

Grave Concerns

Between AD 740 and 1050 Britain was prey to the
Viking raiders who sailed the North Sea in longboats
decorated with dragon heads. These fierce Scandina-
vians landed on our eastern coast, then travelled far
inland, looting, raping and burning as they went and
often wiped out whole communities.

Balsham in south-east Cambridgeshire was not
immune from assault. With the exception of one man,
the entire settlement was wiped out during a Viking
incursion in the 11th century, led by the fearsome
Danish leader Svend Forkbeard. He, they said, made
'all England quake before him like a reed bed rustling
in the wind.' During the raid the sole survivor sought
refuge in the doorway to the tower of Holy Trinity
church, where he withstood remorseless attack. Eventually, frustrated by his courage, the foreign horde
was forced to retreat. Miraculously, both man and
building were undamaged and the event is today por-
trayed on the village sign.

Balsham church was also the setting for an incident
which reputedly took place in the middle of the 19th
century. One winter's night some drinkers in the local
tavern were gossiping and laughing uneasily over the
news that the sexton had unearthed some human
remains whilst digging a grave that morning.
Although a common enough occurrence in this
ancient graveyard, it never failed to unsettle the ima-
ginative. As more ale was swallowed the men rois-
tered and larked about, with one of them eventually
throwing down a challenge. He wagered that none
was brave enough to go out in the dark, jump into
that open grave and retrieve an old bone or two

before the next burial was due to take place two days hence.

Not surprisingly there was no immediate uptake, but a few more swallows of good foaming ale loosened the tongue of Giles Smith. He volunteered to go down at eight o'clock on the following night, which would be a miracle in itself for he was past his 80th birthday, poor sighted and stiff with rheumatism. However, bets were laid and secret plans hatched behind the old man's back which produced winks, nudges and stifled laughter from the knowing.

These pranksters crept into the churchyard at half past seven the next night and hid behind a tombstone close to the open grave. They did not have long to wait until Giles shuffled up, carrying a spade in one hand and a candle stuck in a jam jar in the other. He lowered himself uneasily into the hole, then began his gruesome search. The watchers in the shadows tiptoed out of hiding to watch their crony, who by now was digging away like a Jack Russell on the scent of a ferret.

Time passed, then he found what he was seeking. It was a piece of skull. 'Gotcha me ol' beauty!' he cried.

'Now you put that down, Giles,' said one of the onlookers in as weird and ghostly a voice as he could manage. 'It's mine, not yours!'

Giles showed no signs of fear. 'I says put it back,' commanded the one from above. 'It's my 'ead and I needs it!'

'Now I knows that in't strictly true,' replied the scavenger without raising his eyes. 'I think's you's tellin' me a bit of a lie, cuz I don't reckon any man's ever 'ad two skulls!'

The joke had back-fired! The old chap was hauled out of the grave and in a right good humour walked with his friends to the public house to sort out the finances. Much later some men returned home richer, others poorer, whilst the hero staggered down the road with money in his pockets and free beer in his belly, grinning broadly as he unknowingly walked into Balsham folklore.

BARNACK

Charles Kingsley and the Button Cap Ghost

Barnack lies to the north of Peterborough, in what was old Northamptonshire. Its famous ragstone quarries provided materials for many East Anglian buildings including abbeys, cathedrals and the Cambridge colleges.

Charles Kingsley, who grew up to be the author of *The Water Babies* and champion of many social reforms, was five years old when he moved with his family to the village in 1824. His father had been ordained parish priest and they lived in the 14th century rectory, since renamed Kingsley House. According to local tradition, when confined to bed with a childhood illness Charles was frequently haunted by a ghost, popularly believed to be a former rector who had cheated a widow and her orphan out of money. The apparition was clothed in a dressing gown and a nightcap with a button on it, hence its name 'Button Cap'!

BARNWELL

Jacob Butler and his House Ghosts

Old Abbey House, in Abbey Road, was built by the Butler family in the 15th century on the site of the former Augustinian priory. Although today in need of some attention, this house which is now divided into apartments still remains beautiful under tall chimneys, Tudor gables and a mellow clay-tiled roof.

Jacob Butler, who was affectionately known as 'Squire', was the last of his family to live there, and his many eccentricities made him an interesting character. Standing 6 feet 4 inches tall, he was a popular, stout barrister-at-law and a lover of good food and drink. Some months before his death in 1765, he took delivery of an enormous oak coffin in which he and his friends would sit, drinking several bottles of brandy at a time! His funeral arrangements stipulated that his remains should be placed in this infamous casket and taken for burial in the Abbey church on an open wagon pulled by his two favourite horses named Brag and Dragon. If this proved unacceptable, he was to be buried in the gardens of Old Abbey House. However, foreseeing all sorts of problems, when the time came the executors of his estate simply had him sealed in a lead shell, which after a dignified service was lowered into the hallowed coffin which had discreetly preceded the deceased to the family vault.

Butler loved animals and when his favourite dog died he supposedly perished from grief. Apparently this pet used to haunt the house, either in its original form or else in the guise of a squirrel known as 'Furry', which sometimes changed into a 'long beaked creature with flippers'! In whatever shape, this bizarre spectre always whined sadly for its adored master. Although it vanished in 1924 when Mass was said by a group of priests who were staying in the house during the Pax Romana Conference held in Cambridge that year, it has been seen in its 'beaky' form walking about Merton Hall at the junction of Queen's Road and Northampton Street. Furthermore, the Scottish wife of a college don, who was gifted with second sight, claimed she saw it playing in the fields by Madingley Road.

The house is also connected with a more commonplace apparition. This is the 'Grey Lady', who was obviously unaffected by the spiritual cleansing in the 1920s and continued to materialise until about 1959. This benign spirit, who many claimed to have seen and who made domestic pets jittery, was thought to be that of a nun from the former Benedictine nunnery of St Radegund, now part of Jesus College. Local tradition has this building linked to Old Abbey House by a secret tunnel, whose entrance lies behind the bricked archway in its vaulted cellar. This afforded the wayward woman easy access to her secret lover, a canon from Barnwell Priory. When their affair was discovered she was walled up alive in this passageway.

Similar stories are told of passages connecting other religious houses to the outside world and their bricking-up is a favoured folkloric ending for nuns who abandoned their vows and trysted their lives away. If the residence of the outrageous 'Squire' could house a three-in-one animal ghost, why not a disgraced holy spirit? Although all remains quiet in Old Abbey House, perhaps the gifted wives of intellectual men who value their credibility should continue to avoid using Madingley Road!

BARTON

The Knocking Ghost of Barton

The undated manuscript of this song of the mischievous ghost which once troubled the Barton area and outwitted the university, comes from the local history section of Cambridge Central Library. Unfortunately the music is not included.

> 'Oh, have you heard the news of late –
> About the knocking ghost so great,
> Oh, if you've not 'tis in my pate,
> About the ghost near Barton.
> Its knocking caused such alarm –
> At the door of Mr H——'s Farm,
> Although it does no other harm;
> They say it is a gypsy's charm;
> They've tried to find out all they can,
> Whether it's a woman or a man,
> But it deceives them in their plan,
> Does this knocking ghost near Barton.

(Chorus)
> Jiminy, criminy, what a lark,
> You must not stir out after dark,
> For if you do you'll get a mark –
> From this knocking ghost of Barton.

> In Cambridge it has caused such fun,
> That men, and boys, and children run,
> With pistols, swords, and likewise gun,
> To kill the ghost near Barton.
> The Collegians too, though learned men,
> Cannot find out the where and when,
> In fact, we know not where will end,

The knocking of this unearthly fiend;
It's knocking there both night and day,
It terrifies them every way,
Yet it wants nothing – so they say,
This knocking ghost near Barton.

Jiminy, criminy &.

It puts old women in a fright,
They dare not stir out day or night,
Yet still there's nothing comes in sight –
Of this dreadful ghost near Barton.
It's frightened people by its wits,
It's drove policemen into fits,
And licks the doctor all to bits,
By loud thundering, knocking hits;
They don't know how to find it out,
Nor how the knocking came about,
But still there's plenty have their doubt –
Of this knocking ghost near Barton.

Jiminy, criminy &.

The turnpike-man is nearly crazed,
He says he dare not keep his place,
For fear to see the ugly face
Of this naughty ghost near Barton.
The people cannot get no rest,
The knocking it is such a pest,
Although some treat it as a jest;
It is a bore I must confess
To have a ghost come night and day,
And knock, knock, knock, in such a way,
I wish they would the devil pay –
This ugly ghost near Barton.

Jiminy, criminy &.

It's no respect of person's pay,
For it was but the other day,
It frighten'd a carter, so they say,
Did this naughty ghost of Barton.
On the Madingley road this ghost did roam,
And stop his horses coming home,
And now he dare not go alone;
He's been laid up two day at home.
On East Road it has found its way,
This ghost it often goes astray,
At Mr P's it found its way,
Did this wicked ghost of Barton.

Jiminy, criminy &.

But now I must my song conclude,
And I hope the ghost won't be so rude,
As any further to intrude,
And frighten folks at Barton.
For if he do, as sure as fate,
He will repent when it's too late,
He'll get a crack upon his pate,
Which if he does will lay him straight;
Take my advice leave off your tricks,
Or you will get into a fix,
By frightening people into fits,
And go no more to Barton.

Jiminy, criminy &.'

THE BEDFORD LEVEL

The Crow Witch

During the early years of the 20th century, night travellers passing by the 'Witch's Hole' which lies
against the Hundred Foot Drain on the Bedford Level

16

might still have heard the ghostly cries of protest from Flora, who was buried alive there on a charge of witchcraft. This is her story.

During the reign of Charles I, the fourth Earl of Bedford, who owned a large estate at Thorney near Peterborough, embarked on an ambitious drainage project masterminded by the Dutch engineer, Cornelius Vermuyden. He was joined in the project by 13 'Gentlemen Adventurers' and had the backing of the King. The return on their investment would be 95,000 acres of reclaimed land to be called the 'Bedford Level'.

The undertaking began in 1630 and took place in two stages, its progress interrupted by the Civil War. Vermuyden's ambitious plan was the cutting of the 21 mile long parallel Old and New Bedford rivers, the latter also known as the Hundred Foot Drain, stretching from Earith to Salters Lode in Norfolk. The Fen people greeted the whole project with dismay, especially the 'Fen Slodgers' who lived out in the wet and made a living from wildfowling and fishing. Since there was no willing local labour force, the unpopular Huguenot and Walloon navvies who had recently completed work on Vermuyden's North Lincolnshire project were brought in and colonised at Thorney. Over the years Dutch and French prisoners of war were also commandeered to dig out the drainage system.

The insular and suspicious Fen dwellers hated strangers and made murderous plans which earned them the name 'Fen Tigers'. They turned as cunning and dangerous as jungle cats, persistently vandalising the newly dug rivers and dykes, smashing the sluice gates and killing the diggers, whose bodies were buried in the river banks. However, the 'Tigers' were loyal to each other. If one was in trouble he or she had only to whisper a secret password and hand over a split grey goose-feather and help had to be given by the recipient, no matter what the personal consequence. Even today, if you call a born and bred Fenlander a 'Fen Tiger' you will probably be thanked for the compliment, so proud are they of their forebears' struggle for their way of life.

However, despite their tenacity over the years many protesters were hunted down and hanged for their crimes. Although work was halted during the English Civil War, the subsequent presence of Matthew Hopkins, the Witchfinder General, contributed to a permanent legacy of bitterness. With his partner John Stearne, in 1645 and 1646, he was active in flushing out the so-called witches of the Fens and fanned already inflamed passions. Perhaps understandably, these dreadful times spawned a climate of superstition and vindictiveness that ended in a witch's screams out on the lonely Bedford Level.

Robert McKinder was a Scottish prisoner of war taken at the Battle of Dunbar in 1650 who had been forced to work on the drainage project. In time, he could have gone home, but he stayed on and his wife Flora joined him. They bought a small tavern, which is said to have stood on the site of the old pumping station on the Welney to Little Downham road, within the shadow of the Hundred Foot Drain. Rob distilled a cheap rough whisky, which encouraged neighbours to look kindly on him and Flora. Business was brisk until he was unfortunately killed when his still exploded.

Without the whisky, trade went down and so one morning his widow, Flora, was delighted to see in the distance a party of strangers heading her way. Believing some Scottish music would help undo their purses, she reached for her husband's bagpipes. However, the leader of the group was enraged when his horse, frightened by Flora's racket, reared up and threw him in the dyke which lay alongside the tavern. Worse still, he turned out to be King Charles II, who had both a political and financial interest in the drainage of the Fens and was planning to build a palace on newly created land at Manea. The King had a nickname of 'Old Wag' and for many years this dyke was called 'Wag's Ducking'.

The King, wet and humiliated, ordered Widow McKinder to be thrashed to within an inch of her life and her tavern burned to the ground. He continued his journey whilst his men obeyed their orders, finally leaving their victim for dead. However, she survived and her ordeal transformed her into a hunchbacked simpleton. With nowhere to live, she walked the Bedford Level, living rough and begging.

It was not long before this now dirty, friendless woman became a social outcast, especially when she tamed a crow to sit upon her left shoulder. The Fenlanders disliked her and dubbed this poor soul the 'Crow Witch'. They accused her of many wicked acts of witchcraft, including responsibility for the Bishop of Ely's rheumatic knees. In the end, superstitious people fuelled with mischievous gossip took her and almost drowned her in the Hundred Foot Drain, before killing her bird.

Time passed with Flora living in the shadows, keeping her head down and dodging the Fen Tigers. However, not long after the draining work on the Bedford Level was completed, there was a torrential storm which lasted many days and nights. Water streamed down from the uplands into the new rivers. The Hundred Foot Drain swelled until its banks were breached and the brown spewing water totally devastated the land and drowned many people and animals. This dreadful storm was generally agreed to be the work of the Scottish woman, especially since she happened to be one of the few survivors! So, after the flood water receded she was again dragged to the river bank, but this time she was fastened to chains and thrown across the open breach in the bank, where she was slowly buried alive, all the while screaming her innocence.

The place where she died became known as the 'Witch's Hole', and here within memory, lone travellers claimed to hear her ghostly cries and the noise of rattling fetters echoing across the level.

BUCKDEN

Dick Turpin at the George Hotel

Buckden is a beautiful old Huntingdonshire village set on the original route of the Roman Ermine Street or Great North Road. At one time this thoroughfare was the most important in England, linking London with York, and Buckden was a stopping place for the coaching trade. The 17th century George Hotel was a principal inn, bustling with ostlers scurrying to arrange a change of horses whilst tired wayfarers sought comfort in the hostelry.

This busy road was plagued with highwaymen, including Dick Turpin. Born in 1706 and hanged at York on 2nd April 1738, this son of a shady Saffron Walden butcher would have remained a forgotten pox-marked thief, murderer and rapist had not the writer J. Harrison Ainsworth placed him in a best-selling novel entitled *Rookwood* which was published in 1834. It was he who transformed this mean crook into a swashbuckling hero seated astride a fictitious horse called 'Black Bess'. Following the novel's success and perhaps with an eye to trade, tales of his ghost were soon being told in many of the old hostelries flanking the Great North Road, now partially re-routed and designated the A1.

Dick often visited the George Hotel, and a black-coated figure wearing a tricorn hat sometimes glides along the first floor corridor, where he always stayed in what is now '106 Turpin's Room'. Apparently the hatchway in the outside wall opposite this chamber was his preferred escape route whenever the law closed in. Now stuck fast with paint, then it gave access to the sloping roof, down which he slid directly onto the back of Black Bess, who presumably sensing trouble had already left the stable to await her master's descent.

However, Turpin does not have sole claim to the supernatural at the George. Perplexing other-worldly incidents have also been reported in rooms 100, 104, 105 and 112, with some recently verified by members of staff. Doors have unlocked themselves, and an invisible heavy-footed intruder sits on beds, lifting the covers and tweaking the occupants' legs. Not long ago a mother sleeping alongside her young daughter in the latter room claimed to have been awoken by the child, who was fully conscious and speaking in a gruff male voice. Utterly convinced that it was some malevolent spirit manifesting itself through her child, she foreshortened their stay and left the following morning. These allegations would suggest that in this oldest part of the building nightmare scenarios can become a reality for a few visitors. However, with the exception of the main staircase which on occasion is used by a spectral woman, the rest of this comfortable hotel is reassuringly peaceful.

The Ghost of Queen Catherine

Catherine of Aragon was the ardently Catholic first wife of Henry VIII and is said to haunt the episcopal palace at Buckden, which from the 12th to the 19th centuries belonged to the Bishops of Lincoln. The sole survivor of Henry and Catherine's six children was a girl, Mary, but the King demanded a son and heir. When Catherine was past childbearing years he forsook her in favour of Anne Boleyn. Because Catherine would not agree to a divorce she was incarcerated at Buckden Palace. However, such was the public sympathy for the jilted Queen, the King decided to move her from alongside this great thoroughfare to a more isolated spot.

Catherine dismissed this proposal so eventually the Duke of Suffolk was dispatched to forcibly shift her. Seeking refuge in a small room to the rear of the chapel, she locked the door and despite Suffolk's dire threats would not meet his demands. Meanwhile a large angry mob had gathered outside the gatehouse, yelling for his blood should their Queen be harmed. Wisely the King's man left empty handed, except for a few personal possessions belonging to the Queen. Although her bolt hole has no connection with her death, her spectre is said to materialise in this appropriately named 'Haunted Room'.

Queen Catherine spent a year at Buckden before eventually agreeing to transfer to nearby Kimbolton Castle, where she died from natural causes in 1536. Most of that time was spent in the tiny 'Queen's Room' located in the south wing, and both this and the main staircase are reputedly haunted by her presence. The castle is now a public school.

Catherine's body was later taken from Kimbolton and interred in Peterborough Cathedral. In 1643 Cromwell's men destroyed her tomb and the replacement black marble memorial slab was financed in the 1890s from donations of sixpences given by women and girls named Catherine.

BURNT FEN

The Bad Witch Blues

During the 19th century a witch called Mrs Kemp lived with 24 cats in this small hamlet close to Littleport. Although black is usually associated with her craft, she preferred blue and wore ragged clothes in every shade, hidden beneath a patina of filth. This is why until fairly recent times many superstitious local women refused to wear blue, which they associated with bad luck.

Mrs Kemp was five times married, with each husband dying soon after the wedding. When this story begins she was preparing for the sixth, but the wedding never took place for her intended died in mysterious circumstances following his stag night party. Not only is it astonishing that any man should desire this infamous woman, but that he could muster sufficient friends to celebrate his good fortune is beyond credulity. However, he had set off to walk home alone beside the drainage channel and was not seen again until a week later, when the stoker at the pumping station fished his bloated body writhing with eels from the water.

Although it was never determined whether his death was accidental or deliberate, Mrs Kemp demanded a scapegoat and cursed the inoffensive stoker who had found him. A few weeks later the poor chap was killed in an accident at work, but the virago's wrath was unappeased. All who subsequently took his job came to grief and it was not long before the pumping station was abandoned.

Although now mainly computerised and unmanned, these pumps still play a vital role in the drainage of the Fens, for the water from the low-lying areas has to be lifted into the higher main water channels which flow to the sea. In Mrs Kemp's day they were steam-driven and the boiler stoker's job paramount. Therefore, according to the story, this witch in blue was responsible for the fertile land around Burnt Fen becoming waterlogged and useless. Her fury continued unabated. She plagued people with 'Fen Ague', better known as malaria for the disease-carrying mosquito of the *Anopheles* genus still thrived in this wet environment. She infected children with chicken pox, sent disease to cattle and fever to the swine, finally driving this small community into taking desperate action.

Late one night when she must surely have been asleep, a gang of men tip-toed up her path, barred her door from the outside, then burnt the house to the ground. But the next day the bad-tempered woman was very much alive, and nobody believed Sam Gotobed who claimed to have seen her and the 24 cats over at Westmoor Common on the night of the fire.

Now homeless, but considered indestructible, Mrs Kemp and her felines moved closer to Littleport where they occupied a shack near the present White Hall Farm. Every night she crept out in the dark to squeeze the udders of startled cows whose milk squirted into two dozen wide open mouths! One night the angry farmer lay in wait and shot 23 of the plump cats, before turning the bull out on their mistress. To no avail, for she was said to have then avenged herself by killing him and his family.

The 'witch' died two years after this incident. Where she was buried remains a mystery, but they had tied bricks around the necks of her cats and thrown them in the river, just in case they too had magic powers. It was not long before the pumping station was reopened and good times returned to Burnt Fen, but the superstitious continued to shun the colour blue. It was far too 'Mrs Kemp' for them.

CAMBRIDGE

College Hauntings – Jesus College

Cambridge University is almost 800 years old and many of its colleges are reputed to be haunted, including Jesus College founded in 1496 by John Alcock, Bishop of Ely. Its oldest buildings formed part of a nunnery built circa 1133 and dedicated to the virgin St Radegund. Leading from the stone floor in the angle of the cloister adjoining the Hall is an extremely steep staircase formerly called 'Cow Lane', now 'G' staircase. This is the route to the infamous 'Ghost Room', which following the last meeting of the Everlasting Club held there on 2nd November 1766 was considered unfit for human habitation and remained firmly padlocked for some 200 years.

This club, modelled on the Hellfire Club, was founded in the 18th century by the Hon Alan Dermot, the hedonistic son of an Irish peer. Membership was both corporeal and incorporeal (in life and death) and limited to seven: himself, Charles Bellasis, Henry Davenport, Francis Witherington, James Harvey, William Catherston and one other. The behaviour of these 'Everlastings' aged between 22 and 30 years was totally degenerate. One was a Fellow-Commoner of Trinity, three were Fellows of other colleges, another a Fellow of Jesus College, one a landed gentleman and the seventh a Cambridge physician.

Between 1738 and 1743 accounts of their meetings were recorded in a minute book, in which each member signed his name and entered his address. Arthur Gray, Master of Jesus from 1912 to 1940, included the story of the club in his anthology of college ghosts, and said that although this book came into the possession of a predecessor, it probably no longer exists.

The Annual Meeting, the most degenerate event of the year, was held at 10 pm every All Souls' Day, the 2nd November, with each member taking his turn to host the event in his place of residence. When the high-spirited Alan Dermot signed the book on 2nd November 1743 his companions were completely unaware that five days earlier he had been killed in a duel in Paris, and according to the rules was now an incorporeal member! When they realised they had been roistering with a ghost, 'they left Cambridge and buried themselves in widely parted regions.' None wished to continue with the Annual Meeting, but were obliged by the club rules to meet every October to put their objection in writing.

Over the next 23 years all except Charles Bellasis died, and on 18th May 1766 he recorded in the minute book that he was the only remaining corporeal member. Now a sober Fellow of Jesus College, with the scandal of his younger days unknown to the new generation of students and long forgiven by his contemporaries, he lived in the college at the top of the 'Cow Lane' staircase. Although he was alone in his room on the night of 2nd November that year, at 10 pm all hell broke loose. For two hours many heard the sound of crashing glass, breaking furniture, bawdy songs, swearing and blaspheming. Not even the Master dared to enter Bellasis' chamber. However, peace returned at midnight, and when workmen eventually smashed the lock on the sturdy oak door the following morning they discovered seven chairs placed around the table. Six were overturned, and in the other sat the remaining 'Everlasting', who was dead.

That night the final entry had been made in the minute book. Six 'Everlastings' had signed their names, but none had given their addresses.

Although this room was turned into a store and remained locked and disused for almost two centuries, at 10 pm each All Souls' Day (a time traditionally associated with ghosts and spirits) the raucous din of the 'Everlastings' could be heard from behind its stout door. Then there was peace and in 1924 the room was converted back into living quarters and has been corporeally occupied ever since.

Corpus Christi College

Founded in 1352, this is one of the smallest and oldest of the Cambridge colleges. One of several Corpus Christi ghosts is said to be that of the gentle Dr Butts, Vice-Chancellor of the University who became the Master of Corpus Christi in 1626.

In 1630 Cambridge was beset by plague and Dr Butts wrote to Lord Coventry, High Steward of Cambridge, describing the plight of the town, for which as a principal figure, he felt a large share of responsibility. Butts became more and more dejected and on Easter Day, 1st April 1632 the pulpit in Great Mary's church from which he always preached stood empty. Aware of his depression, a frantic search was made of Corpus Christi and he was found hanging by the neck in his rooms above the kitchens in Old Court.

For many years following his suicide his ghost was seen, with a huge red gash about its neck, haunting these very rooms. It was always at a time when a college member was either seriously ill or in extreme danger.

Another spectre, also reputed to be of that period, is that of Elizabeth, the daughter of Dr William Spencer, Rector of Landbeach near Cambridge and Master of Corpus Christi from the 1630s to 1693.

For several years young Elizabeth had been embroiled in a secret love affair, using the kitchens in the old Lodge as a trysting place. One day the lovers were disturbed. With no time to spare she hid her paramour in a wooden chest, where he died of suffocation. We are not told when she died, but her death was not peaceful. Elizabeth Spencer haunted these rooms until their conversion into living quarters in 1825, frightening any servants who were working after dark.

A curious incident which allegedly occurred in rooms opposite these former kitchens was reported in an article in the *Occult Review* of March 1905, as quoted by Edith Porter in her book *Cambridgeshire Customs and Folklore*.

'In the Easter term of 1904 an undergraduate ... who had rooms opposite those said to be haunted, happened to come in at three o'clock in the afternoon, and as soon as he had sat down to work, found himself seized with a curious feeling of uneasiness, which made it impossible for him to concentrate his mind. He got up and, looking out of the window, noticed the head and shoulders of a man leaning out of a window of the upper set of rooms opposite. The features, he was rather surprised to find, he could not recognise: they were those of a stranger with long hair, who remained perfectly motionless, and seemed to glare down upon him. For three minutes he stood at the window and watched, and then, thinking he might see better from his bedroom, he ran there, but by the time he had arrived, the man opposite had completely disappeared.

'The young man was now thoroughly excited and went across the court to the upper set of rooms opposite. However, he found the door locked, and when he called no answer was given. In the evening, after careful enquiry he discovered that the owner of the rooms had been out the whole afternoon, and that it was quite impossible that anyone could have been in the rooms from the time of his departure at two o'clock to the arrival of his bedmaker at half-past six.'

After the apparition had been seen again on subsequent occasions the occupier of the rooms 'made up his mind to try to exorcise it, and got C—, a friend from another College, who was interested in spiritualism, to come to his rooms for the purpose, with four other men.

'At the outset they all knelt down, said the Lord's Prayer, and called upon the Three Persons of the Trinity to command the spirit to appear. It was then seen, but only by two of the six men. Another said that he felt a peculiarly cold and chilling air, but the rest saw nothing. The two who saw the ghost – the man interested in spiritualism and the occupant of the rooms – describe it as appearing in the form of a mist of about a yard wide, which slowly developed into the form of a man who seemed to be shrouded in white, and had a gash in his neck, and that it then moved slowly about the room. The two men got up, and, holding the crucifix in front of them, approached the apparition, but seemed to be forced back by some invisible agency. They cried out, "It drives me back", and then both completely broke down, becoming quite unnerved.

'A few days later they tried to exorcise the spirit,

with exactly the same result; the same men saw it, and no one else. They were again driven back, although this time they approached holding hands. The others allege that they appeared to grow stiff, and that they gripped one another convulsively. The meeting was again broken up without anything definite having been effected.'

Geoff Yeates gives a fuller and more chilling account in his book *Cambridge College Ghosts*. Several undergraduates witnessed the commotion which accompanied the exorcism and he says the college authorities tried to hush things up and temporarily closed the haunted rooms. It took an American who struck a deal to live in them rent free to restore the status quo, even if it did not stop the Sunday trippers from congregating under the notorious windows, hoping to catch a glimpse of the ghostly occupant.

CAXTON GIBBET

The Dastardly Landlord

In 1994 the Caxton Gibbet public house changed hands and became the Caxton Gibbet Chinese Restaurant. Situated close to the Cambridge and Royston crossroads, it now looks rather incongruous, placed as it is alongside an old replica of a former gallows. The iron gibbet cage, in which the criminal's body would be displayed after death, is missing, but one would have swung from its arm, with its decaying occupant being a gruesome reminder to all would-be criminals. Somehow, an English pub looked far more in keeping with such an abhorrent historical reminder, standing together out on a lonely wind-swept rise yet within the sound of heavy traffic.

The original hostelry, for this building too is a replacement, was built sometime in the 18th century as a convenient stopping point for wayfarers travelling these two busy roads. It also offered refreshment for the morbid, who flocked around the gibbet after a public execution. According to a story which for years was displayed on a board over the fireplace in the main bar, a certain landlord of the Caxton Gibbet committed a murder most foul. When I asked the new owner where the board had gone he told me that it was stored in London, for he feared it might put his patrons off their food. I can see his point, but fortunately I can remember the gist of the tale from a previous visit.

Once upon a time the pub was owned by a scurrilous landlord who at the drop of a hat would pick a fight with anyone. He was a cheat, a Sabbath breaker and worse. One night three wealthy gentlemen travellers booked lodgings in this hostelry and, being an accomplished thief who habitually stole from his customers, the wicked landlord made plans.

The three men shared a room and when they were fast asleep their host crept in to rifle through their baggage and pockets. Suddenly one of them awoke and cried out, only to be killed by the publican. The other two were roused by the commotion and so he killed them too, to avoid swinging from the gallows tree next door. That was the easy part, but finding a place to hide their bodies was more difficult. He settled for the well, dragged the men one at a time down the path, threw them in and replaced the lid. The next morning he pretended they had left without settling their account.

As cadavers and drinking water do not mix, nature took her course and brought the crime to light. The

31

perpetrator ended up in the iron gibbet cage, slowly rotting away until his bones rattled their warning in the wind which scuds across this bleak point. His spectre is said to haunt the building, but hopefully it has now vanished along with the storyboard.

CHATTERIS

The Wandering Toadman

This tale embraces an agricultural practice which was fairly common in parts of East Anglia until the beginning of the 20th century. Such was the importance of the working horse on the land that some horsemen allegedly gained complete mastery over their animals by selling their souls to the Devil. This ensured their skills were always in demand; however, they paid the ultimate price when they died because they went straight to Hell. They were called 'Toadmen'.

Their reputed magical powers were gained from undergoing a lonely ritual. The initiate had to kill a natterjack toad under the full moon at midnight, leave its body on a thorn bush or buried in an ant heap until its flesh was picked clean, then throw the skeleton into a fast moving stream, again at the witching hour in the same moon quarter. A trance-like watch had to be kept on the toad's remains, for at some stage one particular bone was said to break free and float away with the current. Once this bone was snatched from the water and placed in his pocket, the newly empowered Toadman would have an uncanny way with horses until he chose to discard his talisman, usually by burying it in a deep hole. This was probably when the thought of the

Devil claiming his soul when he died became too much to bear.

However, according to this story which a very old lady shared with me, the newly deceased had to make a journey deep under ground to ask the worms to eat their bodies, for unless they were totally consumed they would turn into ghosts. This was her favourite childhood tale, about Elijah the Ghostly Toadman. It was told by her grandfather, who reckoned his father had seen this spectre on the farm where he worked, out in the lonely Acre Fen on the road to Somersham.

According to him, the farmer had engaged Elijah at a Michaelmas Hiring Fair and let him live in a wooden hut or bothie which stood close to the straw stackyard. He was an excellent ploughman and skilled at keeping the horses in good condition. The farmer was notoriously mean and always making excuses for delaying paying the wages, so after a few months Elijah decided to teach him a lesson. One day when working with the horses he whispered something into the ears of the large, gentle creatures which rooted them to the ground, and he claimed they would stay there until he was paid, even if it took a year. The master swore and tugged at their reins but could not move them an inch, so had no choice but to stump up the money he owed. After this, bad feeling grew between the two men. One night the resentful farmer crept into the bothie and, Elijah being a heavy sleeper, removed his right thumbnail with a pair of pliers. The Toadman swore and cussed, but took no revenge.

Tempers eventually simmered down, until the master accused him of stealing some rashers of fat bacon which several witnesses had seen the dog eat. The disbelieving farmer ranted and raged, and that night again stole upon the sleeping man and chopped

33

his right arm off at the shoulder with a big axe! Then, feeling a bit guilty, he offered to give Elijah a few days' sick leave if he promised not to go to the law or perform any more horse magic. Surprisingly, Elijah agreed to the proposition!

Two nights later the farmer was awoken by an uncommonly bright sky. The barn was on fire and his first thoughts were of his horseman. Crazed with rage and still in his nightshirt he rushed down to the bothie, grabbed its snoring occupant by the throat, dragged him across the yard and flung him into the fire where he roasted like a pig.

The old lady who told me this story then explained that if the dead were to rest in peace, at the point of death they must make their way underground to be eaten by the worms, otherwise they will turn into ghosts. Elijah had a problem because he was just a pile of ashes strewn about the farm, but some part of him managed to make the journey. He confronted the Chief Worm who said he could not be consumed because there was no corpse to eat! Elijah explained the cause of his death, but the worm was adamant. No corpse, no obligation! Then it relented. If Elijah could retrieve his ashes, the worms would eat them. So he went back to Chatteris and after much investigation put his bits and pieces in a stout sack and returned to the Chief Worm who greeted him cordially. The creature crawled into the sack, investigated its contents and reported something was missing.

'That will be my arm,' said the Toadman. 'The farmer chopped it off, but I don't know where he put it.'

However, rules were rules in this strange underworld. The dead man was sent back to Chatteris and the severed limb was retrieved, but the Chief Worm was still not satisfied. There was the question of the missing thumbnail! Elijah begged the worm to over-look this tiny loss which would be impossible to find, but the slimy one was adamant. Until everything was found he would have to remain a ghost.

This, according to my informant's great grand-father, is what happened, for on occasion he and others had seen the one-armed Toadman bathed in an eerie green light scrutinising the land in that remote location. Perhaps after years of looking he found what he was seeking, for the 'Wandering Toadman' has not materialised for a long while. As for those who thrilled to his story, most are dead and buried in peaceful churchyards.

CHESTERTON

The Naming of Stourbridge Common

This piece of open land lies against the river Cam a few miles from the centre of Cambridge. It is pro-nounced 'Stirbitch' Common and according to folk-lore, this is how it got its unusual name.

Some centuries ago, there was a tinker called Mumper who was well known locally and lived rough with his dog Bess. Together they would walk miles, he mending pots and pans, dealing, diddling and cadging off those with money and food to spare; Bess simply devoted to her canny master. Mumper was very old and his dog too was becoming stiff and white of whisker. After walking over from Newmar-ket on a particularly hot summer's day, they rested in the shade of a willow standing on public land along-side the river Cam.

Both were utterly exhausted and so they slept

35

soundly for three days and three nights. When Mumper eventually awoke, he was horrified to see Bess lying there as still as death. He stroked her, he prodded her, but still she would not budge. Finally, he stood up and commanded, 'Stir, bitch, stir!', whereupon Bess immediately sprang into action and licked him all over.

Two workmen happened to witness the event. They swore that the dog really had come back to life and so it was agreed that the spot, which had no name, should be called 'Stirbitch Common'. But the clerk could not spell and so it became Stourbridge!

COLERIDGE

The Ghost Train

In 1985 Michael Moore, then a university technician, took the tenancy of a brand new one-bedroomed first floor council flat in Budleigh Close, Coleridge, an eastern suburb of Cambridge. For several years he lived there undisturbed, with no concerns apart from the snails which climbed determinedly up the outside wall to reach his sitting room. However, these slimy molluscs were nothing compared to what came into his bedroom in January 1990. This travelled at a much quicker pace.

Usually late to bed, Michael could not have been long asleep when he was awoken at about 2 am by a tremendous hissing noise. Instinct made him throw himself against the wall a split second before a ghostly train with a good head of steam thundered past his bed! Frozen into a state of paralysis, he saw its passengers seated in their well lit carriages, swaying and clanking over invisible rails. They were looking straight ahead, oblivious that their journey was taking them through an occupied bedroom!

After the train had disappeared through the wall, leaving no hint of cracked plaster or even a smudge of soot, life returned to Michael's frozen limbs. Surprisingly, he was unafraid. After making a pot of tea he went back to sleep and the next day quizzed his neighbours. Had they heard anything untoward during the night? Had a steam engine passed through their bedrooms? They shook their heads in amazement, probably secretly questioning the sanity of this gentle person, who remains convinced of what he saw on that winter's night.

A train hurtling through your home unnoticed by your adjoining neighbours, in a block of flats situated a long distance from the railway, defies credulity. However, the building does stand on the route of the old 1851 Cambridge to Newmarket line which curved sharply away from the Ely main line at the north end of Cambridge station, running due east through Cherry Hinton and Fulbourn to Six Mile Bottom. This meant the Newmarket trains had to cross four lines in addition to the access to the goods depot. This was a dangerous procedure and a train is believed to have crashed at Coldham Common some two miles from Budleigh Close. A new loop was opened on 16th May 1896 and the old track cleared away between 1920 and 1925. Michael wonders if there is any connection between the crashed train, using the old rail layout, and his weird experience, which heralded the start of various strange phenomena encountered throughout 1990 and to a lesser degree into the present time.

His mother came to stay in the August and as was customary slept in the sitting room. One night she had need of the bathroom and to her horror saw a strange man by its door, staggering about and holding his head as if in pain, before fading away. However, he was not dressed in a railwayman's uniform like the man seen by Michael in the same location, so maybe two spirits haunt this one-bedroomed flat.

There are long periods of peace, then spectral energy builds up causing thick glass ashtrays placed on the coffee table to suddenly break in two or fall to the ground without spilling the ash. Toughened glass saucepans smash spontaneously in the kitchen cupboard and sometimes it sounds as if the kitchen window has been broken, when it is still intact. On occasion a strange sweet smell which defies description wafts over the place, while ornaments and flower arrangements move mysteriously to the other side of the room, sometimes floating through the air. The mobile hanging in the sitting room window will spin round at a terrific rate even when the window is closed and the air still, and tapes have the infuriating habit of spontaneously ejecting themselves from all three of Michael's video recorders.

These paranormal phenomena are not experienced in isolation, for his girlfriend and other visitors also witness these events, which some say could be caused by a poltergeist. However, this does not explain the spectral figures lurking by the bathroom door or the ghostly train, albeit seen only once, which may have been taking its passengers to a destination far beyond the limits of the Great Eastern Railway Company. Although Michael Moore's is the only flat to be affected, it does not bother him unduly, for he is certain these unnatural forces are of no threat to the living.

CROUCH MOOR

The Devilish Bargain

Crouch Moor is not far from Littleport, where during the 19th century starving, unemployed people rioted when profiteering farmers 'fixed' the price of corn and so kept bread at an artificially high price. Perhaps they should have taken heed of the following cautionary tale.

A rich and powerful local farmer was known to hold onto his grain to force up the price of bread. One day he met at Ely market a swarthy, pinched-faced stranger dressed in a black cloak, who enquired if he had any corn to sell. The crafty farmer bragged of his well stocked barns, so the Devil, for that was who it was, accompanied him back to Crouch Moor, where an extravagant deal was struck in favour of the Fenman.

The dark stranger paid him a deposit with the promise of the balance upon collection of the grain in four weeks' time. Threshers worked with little sleep to meet the deadline and on the agreed date the purchaser came with a string of horses and carts to collect his goods. However, when all was loaded and it was time to settle the bargain, 'Old Nick' snapped his fingers and vanished in a whirlwind, taking with him the grain, the farmer, his house, stock and family!

DODDINGTON

The Bloodstained Hand

The original parish of Doddington covered 37,801 acres and was the largest in Cambridgeshire. In the Middle Ages it was the site of a palace of the Bishops of Ely. The beautiful church of St Mary the Virgin, the former mother church of March, is mainly 14th century. One of its rectors, Christopher Tye, was the organist for St George's Chapel, Windsor, who in 1560 composed the music for the carol, *While Shepherds Watched Their Flocks by Night*.

By tradition St Mary's contains a reminder of a long forgotten, wicked lord of the manor. He was a tyrant who ruled with an iron fist and harsh tongue. One day a young servant boy incurred his displeasure and, in a blind fury, was whipped to death by his master. Being such a powerful man his lordship avoided hanging, but he could not escape God's punishment. The Almighty decreed that all his possessions were to bear the mark of a large bloodstained hand to remind all of his dreadful crime. His coat of arms, armoury, china, glass, cutlery, everything he owned was to be branded.

If you search one of the choir stalls in the chancel, which is reputed to have been the despot's family pew, you will find a tiny brown hand-shaped stain, no bigger than your thumbnail. This is said to be the one remaining mark and one which I am informed can change from dark brown to blood red. You may wonder why it is so small. Apparently over the years God has decreased the size and when the stain is totally rubbed away, the sins of the ruthless squire will be forgiven.

ELY

The Man Who Could Not Tell His Bed From a Dunghill

The *Isle of Ely Chronicle* dated 17th November 1866 carried a report about the ghost of Jeremiah Newell, which was haunting Potters Lane, off Broad Street. Although at that time a slum area, the reporter said, 'Its inhabitants are honest, we trust, and their veracity unimpeachable.'

Two weeks before the disturbance Jeremiah, better known as Jerry, drank himself into a stupor at the Royal Oak, which stood on the corner of these two roads. At closing time he made his way to his home in Potters Lane, but seeing a steaming dunghill seems to have mistaken it for his bed and fallen fast asleep on top of it. However, at dawn he was seized with the cramp and died *in situ*. Following a 'crowner's quest' (Fen dialect for 'coroner's inquest'), he was buried with due dignity, which should have been the end of this tragic affair, but it was not. According to the 'unquestionable testimony' of many Potters Lane residents, old Jerry was making 'night hideous' by appearing amongst them.

His ghost was first seen by an elderly woman, who confessed to a neighbour that she was almost frightened out of her wits. Her friend accused her of 'waxing desperate with imagination', but they decided to keep a close watch the next night. Sure enough the perturbed spirit came upon them. One of the women fainted, but the bolder one, who was obviously something of a word-smith, informed the newspaper reporter that she exclaimed there and then:

'O Jerry! O answer me.
Let me not burst in ignorance! but tell

Why thy rheumatic bones, hearted in death,
Have burst their cerements! Why the sepulchre
Wherein we saw thee quietly in-win'd,
Hath op'd its jaws, to cast thee up again!'

The deceased shook his head (perhaps he could not understand a word of what she was saying) and beckoned her to follow him, which she said, 'twasn't a bit likely, and a most indecent thing to require.' Then a cock crowed and the spectre vanished in the sunrise.

The gossips went to work. Several of the more timid residents decided to leave there and then, whilst others begged the priest to perform an exorcism. At the time of going to print this had not been granted, but the voice of the *Isle of Ely Chronicle* declared it should be and, 'when, armed with clerical power he (the exorcist) has driven poor Jerry's ghost back to its sepulchre, there to remain till the crack-o-doom, Potters Lane will be itself again.'

Years later when people no longer kept pigs and had the benefits of indoor plumbing, the dunghill vanished along with the ghost. The lane today gives access to a modern housing estate and is both a moral and sanitary credit to the town! Jeremiah Newell would not recognise the place.

Cromwell's Ghost

Oliver Cromwell was born at Huntingdon on 25th April 1599. His grandfather, Sir Henry Cromwell, known as the 'Golden Knight', was the tithe collector for the Dean and Chapter of Ely, and responsible for collecting every tenth sheaf of corn from the fields of the Isle of Ely and beyond. Oliver succeeded him as Steward and for a time lived in the timbered Steward's

42

House situated in St Mary's Street, which was later used as a public house and then became first St Mary's vicarage, then 'Oliver Cromwell's House'. It is now a museum containing his death bed effigy, and also accommodates the city's Tourist Information Centre.

The man who became Lord Protector of England, better known in these parts as 'Old Noll', was well supported within the Isle of Ely, being almost a Fenman himself. He may have led a troop of his Ironsides into the cathedral during Holy Communion to drive out the priest and the communicants, but at least he spared this glorious building which looms out of the haze like a fairy tale castle.

His ghost is said to haunt many parts of Cambridgeshire, including 'Oliver Cromwell's House'. On 29th April 1979, when it was still a vicarage, a visiting canon and his wife were the guests of the incumbent and they were given separate rooms. She had to get up in the night to use the bathroom and upon returning to bed saw a ghostly man walk toward her through the wall. The canon's wife was unafraid, even when the spirit gripped her fiercely by the arms and whispered, 'I mean you no harm. It is not my way.' She pushed it aside, noticing that it was wearing a leather jerkin and its face was remarkably like Cromwell's. Then it returned through the wall without trace.

The following morning the canon inquired if she had slept well and learned of 'Cromwell's ghost', which his wife believed could only have been a nightmarish dream. However, when dressing he noticed red marks on her arms, the sort made by strong hands gripping soft flesh. I am told these were also verified by their host and his wife. Later, extensive renovations to the building showed that in Cromwell's time there had been a doorway in the wall of that bedroom exactly where the ghost had been seen.

'Old Noll' is not the only spectre to haunt the place. On several occasions a grey lady has been seen drifting along an upstairs gallery which was added in the 19th century, when the building was used as a public house.

A Spectral Tourist Attraction

The city's most famous ghosts are a group of medieval monks who may be seen on misty autumn nights walking across the park off Broad Street, destined for some long-ago evensong in the cathedral. One of the brethren sometimes breaks rank to fish in an invisible pond. I am advised by the Tourist Board that the best approach for those hopeful to witness this chilling scenario is to walk around the cathedral and past the gallery, where the path meets with the park entrance.

ETTON

The Everlasting Battle

Woodcroft Castle, known also as Woodcroft Manor or Woodcroft House, is a 13th century moated and embattled castle standing in glorious countryside a few miles from Peterborough. It looks peaceful enough today, yet has a sinister reputation, for it is said to be haunted by Dr Michael Hudson, a former chaplain to Charles I. His ghost is accompanied by the spectral sounds of a battle, fought in this building between the Royalists and the Roundheads in 1648 during the English Civil War.

Dr Hudson was fiercely loyal to the King and raised a troop of yeomen to protect the district from Cromwell's men. They made their headquarters in Woodcroft Castle, then in the county of Lincolnshire, from where he and his men launched several successful attacks on the Roundheads billeted at Stamford. In retaliation their commander, Colonel Winters, sent troops headed by his brother-in-law Captain William Smart to storm Woodcroft, but they were outwitted and Captain Smart killed.

Another troop was raised and, now commanded by Colonel Winters himself, they took the Royalists unawares and besieged the castle. The ensuing battle was long and bloody, with the Royalists finally facing defeat. Colonel Winters promised leniency to the few survivors but vowed death to their leader and ordered a thorough search of the building.

By now Dr Hudson had reached the parapet of the battlements, pursued by one of Colonel Winter's soldiers. He lowered himself over the parapet and hung over the side, intending to drop into the moat below, but the enemy was upon him and ordered him to surrender. Although in such a vulnerable position he refused. The soldier leaned over, lifted his sword and cut off Dr Hudson's hands, watching him plummet into the water like a stone. However, Dr Hudson was still alive. With blood spurting from his severed wrists he swam over to the other side of the moat and staggered up the bank, where four Roundheads barred the way. They knocked him to the ground, where one, a 'low-bred shopkeeper from Stamford', cut out his tongue, then killed him.

Dr Hudson's tongue was paraded around the county as a trophy of war and Woodcroft Castle commandeered by the Parliamentarians. However, the chaplain's ghost is said to appear as a perpetual reminder of that dreadful attack, whilst the clash of weapons and agonising screams are the phantom sounds of this everlasting battle.

EYE

The Devil and the Church Spire

Churches are often popular subjects of folklore, and no wonder considering their once awesome presence in the community. Priests preached hellfire and damnation, people lived to the chime of the church clock, Sundays were ruled by pealing bells, and spires pointed heavenwards, a constant reminder of the wrath of God.

It is not known for how long the spire on the parish church at Eye had been leaning over, but by 1980 it was so dangerous that it had to be demolished. Instead of being admired from a distance, St Matthew's church is now condemned to keep a low profile under a stumpy apology of its former glory. According to tradition, this is how the fine old landmark became damaged.

One Sabbath morning prayers were disturbed when Satan shook and rattled the west door, announcing that he had come to collect the most wicked person in Eye and take him or her to Hell. One of the churchwardens turned the key of the west door, but the unwelcome visitor attempted to break it down, cursing and screaming to be let in. Although the nervous parson ordered the congregation to sing hymns to drown out the Devil's rantings, this horned one proved to be louder than fifty 'alleluias' and a hundred 'amens'.

The organ thundered as people sang as never

before, so Old Nick changed tack and proceeded to climb the outside wall, laughing and making dire threats as his cloven hooves scraped and scratched their way to the top. He clambered over the roof, anchoring himself to the spire by curling his long forked tail around its base. There he sat, hurling abuse on the people below, yelling out that the most wicked person in Eye was certainly amongst the congregation.

During the hymn *O Help Us, Lord! Each Hour Of Need*, he suggested that the biggest sinner might be the stout farmer who grew rich on the poverty of his labourers. John Brown looked uncomfortable, yet had no choice but to sing the words 'For still the more the servant hath, the more he shall receive'.

Then came the turn of the voluptuously accommodating Mrs Smith, wife of the ill-humoured schoolmaster, for in *Oh Love Divine How Sweet Thou Art*, the lofty inquisitor demanded to know how many lovers she had taken since her marriage vows. About 50 men in the gathering, including the parson, had the sudden desire to consider their shoes, whilst Lizzie blushed with embarrassment.

The next to receive unwanted attention were the two churchwardens, one who stole from the charity box, the other young girls' virtue. Both were vilified throughout *Not For Our Sins Alone*, whilst the intemperate verger got his come-uppance during Psalm 42, *As Pants The Hart For Cooling Streams*.

'But no,' yelled the Devil, 'I know of a more cunning thief, and I'm coming to get him ... NOW!'

The parson did not wait. With his cassock in full sail he raced down the aisle and tolled the bell for his very life, in the certain knowledge that the Devil hates this sound and will do anything to avoid it. True to form, Old Nick took off like a rocket. Up he flew, quite forgetting that his tail was still wound round the spire, which was yanked out of shape and weakened forever. Not knowing which way to go the crazed demon panicked. This way, that way, round and round, up and down he flew, scared senseless by the Christian bells which resounded over a great distance.

It is well known that fear can do unpleasant things to bowels – the Devil lost control of his and was not wearing britches! Everything and everybody in his line of fire was covered in his black stinking excrement, which fell for a couple of hours until he calmed down and returned to Hell.

The Fens were plastered in filth which stayed for three or four days until the rain washed it away, with one exception. This was the creeping weed *Arssmart Polygonum*, popularly called 'The devil's a—hole', whose habitat is dykes which dry out in the summer. The blackish marks which can be seen on its broad leaves are said to be a reminder of that time long ago, when the Devil messed himself to the sound of St Matthew's bells and ruined the spire forever!

EYNESBURY

The Gentle Giant

James Toller, better known as the 'Eynesbury Giant', died on 4th February 1818 and was buried in the central aisle of the church of St Mary the Virgin. It was thought he would be safe there, it being rumoured that the medical profession had offered bodysnatchers £20 to steal his corpse.

Described as 'a pleasing, good natured country-looking lad' with an average appetite, Toller was an oddity of nature, for he measured 8 feet, 1.5 inches (half an inch taller than is noted on the church inscription). He lived for most of his 21 years with his family in Rectory Lane in this suburb of St Neots. Although his parents and brother were of average stature, his two sisters were also abnormally tall with one measuring 5 feet at the age of seven.

Toller joined a freak show in 1815, exhibiting in London and touring England, sometimes appearing alongside a dwarf named Simon Paap who was only 28 inches tall. A versifier of the time wrote:

'To see him hundreds day by day did throng,
As he from place to place did pass along.
His 'bode uncertain for to think in vain
One place so tall a wonder to contain.
His whole proportion was upright and straight
'Twas eight foot fully and a half in height
Not much in debt to age, his body clean
Up to his stature and not fat nor lean.'

After quitting show business the 'Eynesbury Giant' had a brief spell in the Life Guards, but declining health forced him to leave the army and return home. A gig was custom built with a deep well to take his feet and strangers were amazed when he suddenly stood up to reveal his full height! Being such an oddity the poor chap was never free from public gaze, so the rector offered him the use of his garden where he could spend his final months walking by himself, enjoying a few precious moments of tranquillity. One day he carved his initials on a big chestnut tree, which after his death craftsmen fashioned into the altar table still serving the church which shelters him.

FEN DITTON

A Jolly Good Bustle!

On Sunday, 6th May 1849 a swarm of strangers were in Fen Ditton, all in holiday mood and jostling with villagers to attend morning service at the parish church. It was not devotion that brought them here, but to see the fiddler undergo his public penance.

Edward Smith enjoyed his beer, which invariably loosened his tongue. When inebriated he called people names and imposed his outrageous opinions on others, but his friends knew it was only the beer talking and simply bought him another pint and called for another tune. Then Smith overstepped the mark by questioning the virtue of the rector's wife. The furious preacher had this popular man solemnly condemned by the ecclesiastical authorities to perform public penance in the church and receive his godly punishment. With hindsight this was a bad decision.

A public penance was an ancient form of punishment, enforced by law, to be performed at certain church services until such time as the wrong-doer proved to have realised the error of his or her ways. Back in the early years of the Church punishment was often of great length and might extend to 10, 15 or even 20 years, although five years was the normal time. It required a lot of weeping, genuflexion and grovelling, until the miscreant was considered worthy to once more partake in the general church services. Although this form of humiliation had fallen or was falling into abeyance as long ago as the middle of the 16th century, the law could still be set in motion some 300 years later, as in the case of the tipsy musician.

It has been suggested that as many as 3,000 visitors converged upon Fen Ditton that day in May, fighting and shoving for a pew or at least standing room, some of the unsuccessful even clambering up and breaking in through the clerestory windows. All wanted to see the penitent walking up the aisle clothed in the traditional ankle-length white sheet, and carrying a long white rod. He made his acknowledgement to the minister, repeating after him words to this effect: 'Good people, whereas I have to the great displeasure of Almighty God and the offence of this neighbourhood committed the crime of insulting the rector's wife whilst under the influence of alcohol and stand thereof convicted by my own confession, I am therefore according to Order come hither to make this acknowledgement. I do humbly confess my said fault and am heartily sorry for the same and beseech God to forgive me and you all to join with me in prayers to Almighty God for the assistance of his Holy Spirit, that I offend not in the like again...' After lengthy admonition he had to swear not to commit the crime again and humble himself once more.

However, following the absolution the congregation raised three rousing cheers for the fiddler, catcalled the rector and his wife, then raced off to smash most of the windows in their house. There followed long hours of drunken revelry. Eventually the visitors returned to their own communities, leaving the people of Fen Ditton to give three cheers more to the now 'legless' and vociferous fiddler. Thanks to him the village had enjoyed a day of high excitement – a jolly good bustle!

GRANTCHESTER

Dreaming of the Lost Fiddler

Lord and Lady Archer live in the Old Manor House, which according to legend is linked to the church by an underground tunnel. Long ago it was explored by a fiddler, who with his dog for company, played merry jigs so that his progress could be followed from above. All was well until the music grew fainter, then finally drifted away and neither he nor his pet were seen again. Although their ghosts are said to haunt this passageway, this claim is dismissed by Jeffrey and Mary Archer. Many counties have similar tales and if trading standards had been in force a century or two ago I am sure every fiddle would have been accompanied by the warning, 'Subterranean playing can seriously damage your health!'

However, it is not the lost fiddler who has made Grantchester famous, but its links with the First World War poet Rupert Brooke, who during his Cambridgeshire undergraduate days lodged at Orchard House in 1909 and later at The Old Vicarage. The village is immortalised in his popular poem, *The Old Vicarage, Grantchester*, where at that time the hands of the church clock were stuck at ten to three and he asks if there is honey still for tea.

Brooke refers to the Orchard Tea Garden, next door to the Archers' home, where he enjoyed taking refreshment with his friends under the shade of the fruit trees. I visited the place when researching this story and on that drowsy midweek autumn afternoon was easily drawn into its idyllic associations. A huge board lists past and present famous patrons, but the fiddler's name is missing!

I sat outside sipping and munching deep in

thought, barely noticing the two very respectable middle aged women picking quinces from a nearby tree. Suddenly both came over to tell me in concerned, hushed tones that they really did have permission and were going home to turn their harvest into jelly. I wished them success and wondered if my long black coat and dark glasses gave me the appearance of the fruit police, or worse still that I was an opportunist jam maker who had an accomplice dressed in blue check trousers and a tall white hat waiting at the getaway vehicle ticking over in the car park! However, I was only day dreaming about the lost fiddler, wondering what would happen if an old man with a long beard and dreadful sense of direction suddenly climbed out of the ground clutching a broken fiddle and a dead dog!

GREAT PAXTON

The Pricking of Nanny Izzard

Ann, better known as 'Nanny', Izzard lived with her husband at Great Paxton in the 19th century. Her sharp tongue and skill at making 'magic charms' and simple medicines earned her the reputation of being a witch. She was constantly abused, and the following story which appeared in the 21st May 1808 edition of the *Cambridgeshire Chronicle* is a typical example.

At 9 pm on Saturday 7th May three men broke into the Izzards' house and carried the screaming Nanny into the yard, whereupon three women, aided and abetted by several men, punched her in the right eye and in the right breast, before pricking her body all over with pins and sharp pointed instruments until she was oozing blood. A similar assault was made the following evening. The offenders were taken before the Huntingdon magistrates, bound over to keep the peace and ordered to appear at the next assizes. At the same time, the chairman of the bench pronounced 60 year old Mrs Izzard to be harmless.

The report continues: 'A few weeks before some misguided people accused her of the Black Art and oh! shame to relate it! at this moment, the poor in general of the parishes of Great and Little Paxton, and some of the farmers also, really believe that she is actually a witch – they firmly believe that she bewitched the women who assaulted her – they believe that she afflicted them with grievous fits – they believe that she overturned a cart drawn by three horses and loaded with corn – they believe that she carried five bushels of wheat upon her back from St Neots to Great Paxton, with as much ease as if they had weighed only five pounds – they believe that she has the power of making herself invisible – they believe that she can convey herself from place to place through the air in an instant – they believe that she gives suck to several imps, which they say she employs in her diabolical arts of witchcraft – and what is worst of all, they believe that this poor woman may be assaulted, either by ducking or otherwise, as they think proper, with impunity.

'The writer of this is shocked that notions, so worthy of the very darkest ages of superstition, and barbarism, so repugnant to commonsense and so disgraceful to humanity, should, at this enlightened period, infiltrate the minds of the people of England.'

Nanny's troubles were to continue. At that time the Bell Inn doubled as a grocery shop and when its owner, John Papworth, was out delivering goods his wife was left in charge. Although a regular customer Nanny Izzard was a bad payer, so Papworth took away her credit. A week or two later Mrs Papworth invited her friend Mrs Hook to tea during her husband's absence. Nanny turned up demanding groceries on the slate and when refused allegedly bewitched the grocer's wife, making her go through all sorts of weird antics which included dancing on the tea table and jumping over the cake! Mrs Hook reacted swiftly. Pulling the fancy pin from her hat, she dived at the unwelcome visitor, held her in an arm lock and pricked her all over, trying to draw the spell out with her blood.

Still entranced, Mrs Papworth continued her crazy antics wailing like a banshee, whilst the 'witch' yelled out in agony as Mrs Hook jabbed her furiously in the name of Christianity. At last she broke free and ran home screaming all sorts of threats and obscenities. This was the first of several prickings, after which she fled to a little cottage in the Royal Oak Yard at St Neots. Here, too, the vilification continued. Mrs Izzard was supposed to know instinctively when the vicar was going to have a bird for dinner and would be waiting on his doorstep early in the morning to beg for its innards which she fed to her familiars or helpmates. Her dubious fame apparently went further than these two Huntingdonshire communities, for one of her 'charms' was later exhibited in the Cotswold Witch Museum at Bourton-on-the-Water. Within memory children dared each other to go to Potton Corner at midnight, where they would see her riding on a broomstick, and parents warned that if they misbehaved Nanny Izzard would take them away.

The *Cambridgeshire Chronicle* reporter referred to May 1808 as being 'an enlightened period', yet even today men and women with certain skills and differing lifestyles can still unwittingly weave threads of fear in superstitious minds.

GREAT STAUGHTON

Old Pork and Lard

In the days when the Tavern at Great Staughton was called the Crown Inn, it was said to have had a former butcher for a landlord who went by the glorious name of 'Old Pork and Lard'. Not only had he salted down lumps of meat when in the trade, but also a small fortune which was rumoured to be hidden somewhere in his public house.

A diet of choice cuts of meat and lumps of fat had done this portly chap no harm, for when long past the biblical age of three score years and ten he decided to get married. Although gross in stature and looks he did have three very desirable assets. Extreme age, wealth and no next of kin! After a brief courtship he wedded a beautiful young woman, but infuriatingly still refused to divulge the whereabouts of his nest egg. Confident that it would be easily located in this small house, she set about hastening his death with her voracious sexual demands. He gratified this need for a year or two, then died in the act of fathering his child!

After the funeral his widow searched the place. Floorboards were raised, walls tapped, rooms rummaged to no avail. So she left Great Staughton and forgot about Old Pork and Lard, who by now had turned into an irksome ghost. For a long time his shadowy figure went about the Crown, presumably also trying to locate the money hoard. Furniture and other items were moved around, tipped up, misplaced or broken. Then all was quiet and has remained so for the last 30 years or more and few now seem aware of the story of the ghost of Old Pork and Lard and his hidden treasure.

56

GUILDEN MORDEN

The Ghostly Bell

This village lies in undulating countryside south-west of Cambridge. St Mary's church is built on its highest point and its tower and lofty spire are an impressive landmark.

In 1845, 23 men, women and children emigrated from Guilden Morden to ~~America~~ *Australia*, sailing on the *Cataraqui*. The ship sank on 4th August that year, with no survivors. Although the news took a long time to reach the village, it did not come as a complete surprise, for the church bell had tolled ominously, by itself, at what was found to be the exact time of the disaster.

HEMINGFORD GREY

The House With a Busy Past

The Norman manor built in 1150 by Payn de Hemingford near the river Ouse, on land granted to him by the king, is thought to be the oldest continuously inhabited house in England. A recent owner was Lucy Boston, the author of the popular 'Green Knowe' children's books who died in 1990 aged 97. She was greatly inspired by this once fortified residence, which today is lovingly preserved by her family.

She immediately fell in love with the place when she saw it for the first time in 1915, and said the river Ouse threaded its way through her thoughts for ever more. Following the break up of her marriage in 1935 Lucy travelled Europe, but when war threatened she returned to England, taking lodgings in Cambridge. When a friend mentioned that 'a house with an old front door' was for sale in Hemingford Grey, she immediately thought of the manor, only to be told by the astonished owners when she arrived on their doorstep that they had only discussed the possibility of putting it on the market that very day!

She and her son Peter took possession in 1938, and tongues instantly began wagging in this close knit community two miles south-west of St Ives. This independent, unattached woman had not only bought a house with a sinister reputation, but was probably spying for Hitler! For she had recently returned from Austria, wore a dirndl skirt and then permitted her attic light to shine carelessly over the water during the blackout!

The original Norman manor had comprised only two rooms, the one above reached by an external ladder. The ground floor was used as a store and the upper storey as the living quarters for the Lord of the Manor and his family. Over the years many alterations were made, and in about 1730 the Gunning family doubled the size of the house when their two beautiful daughters, Maria and Elizabeth, married into the aristocracy. However, the extension was totally demolished by fire in 1798, with the old building probably spared by its thick stone walls. Traces of this disaster can still be seen on one wall of the ground floor sitting room. Could this have been an example of the house rejecting change, a strange force that the Bostons would have to reckon with?

Although aware of stories of the manor's link with the paranormal, Lucy had not reckoned on the degree of malevolence centred around what was to become her music room, where stairs led to the attic. Servants refused to use these back stairs and would not enter this room when the place was empty, such was their fear of the brooding spite and ill will contained within. Lucy herself was able to cope with this and more elsewhere, although some visitors found it too disturbing and foreshortened their stay.

Her son and his wife Diana now live at the manor and it was she who told me these tales. One glorious weekend in the spring of 1939 Peter was removing an extra floor from this sinister music room when suddenly an intense premonition of evil washed over his body, pressing in on him from all sides. At first dismissing the sensation, it then became intolerable as if he were releasing something dreadful along with the redundant timbers. He literally ran for his life to the safety of the garden. This feeling of malevolence remained until the wall partitions were removed and the room returned to its original design.

However, there is a pleasant side to Peter Boston's experience. The following summer with the house now restored to its old shape, he was reading peacefully in the sitting room. Gradually there came upon him an awareness of being surrounded by a great gathering of people dressed in clothes of former periods. The phenomenon lasted a few seconds and was as intensely pleasant as the previous year's experience had been wholly evil. He interpreted it as people from the past welcoming the return of their old manor.

I am told Lucy Boston's one regret was that, unlike others, she never saw a ghost in the house. Yet she heard many uncanny noises, including the sound of a stick clattering over the banisters and against the outside wall. She also listened to the phantom flautist who still performs in the music room, where during the Second World War record concerts were provided on a mighty trumpet gramophone for the airmen stationed nearby. Guests sat huddled together on make-shift couches made from mattresses and car seats draped with candlewick bedspreads. One particular day they were feeling dispirited for one of their crew had been killed the night before. However, during the entertainment loud footsteps were heard on the stairs, the door opened and many saw the deceased walk in.

The past is still busy here, inexplicable things do happen, phantom songs are sung and a woman dressed in a long gown continues to haunt the garden. Readers of Lucy Boston's books will recognise the toys in the attic bedroom, standing exactly as described in the *Children of Green Knowe* story, and appreciate the topiary bushes outside which also had their role. You can visit the house by appointment and walk around its grounds in the daytime usually without notice. Most people enjoy the experience, although I am told that some cannot cope when they unwittingly tune into its paranormal energy. But all the foreboding has gone from this beautifully restored house standing by the river which threaded its way through a woman's dreams.

HISTON

Great Big Moses Carter

Moses Carter was a giant of a man, standing 7 feet tall and weighing some 23 stone, yet as gentle as a lamb. Born in 1801, he never married but lived alone at Histon in a rough hut made of brick bats, which were shaped from local clay mixed with roughly chopped straw and left in the sun to dry. He washed himself and his clothes in Dodd's Pond near the Cottenham road and once a week made an enormous steak pudding, which was boiled for several hours in his copper, along with an armoury of rock-hard dumplings! Moses scraped a living from growing vegetables on Histon Moor, pulling the harrow as capably as any Shire horse. The produce was sold from a cart which he pushed around Cambridge and far beyond, striding out in his 'seven league boots' and bellowing in a voice which demanded attention.

Each year this 'Histon Giant' was a popular attraction in the boxing ring at the Stourbridge Fair, when the public were given the opportunity to fight him, although few remained standing after the third round. He was equally famous for taking on wagers which involved incredible feats of strength. Huge boulders, hundredweights of wheat tucked under each arm, they were nothing to this cheerful sort who was especially good with children. However, this did not deter their mothers from using him as a bugbear when they were naughty. 'Do that again and Moses Carter will chop off your head and replace it with a cabbage!'

Although he died in 1860, aged 59 years, until well after the Second World War boys who were big for their age were still being teased that they were 'getting as big as Moses Carter!'

HORSEHEATH

Bonnie, Blue Cap, Red Cap, Jupiter and Venus

The belief that witches and wizards kept familiars or imps whom they trained to perform evil deeds upon demand, was carried into the 20th century. These creatures were said to assume the appearance of animals and insects such as dogs, cats, birds, mice, spiders and cockroaches, which irrespective of size were kept hidden between their mistress's breasts or in her vagina. Wizards used the anus. These familiars were nourished by their owner's blood, drawn from any bump or pimple on his or her body, known as 'the devil's nipple' and from which Satan also suckled! Some witches and wizards received Holy Communion each Sunday, but kept the Host in their mouths to feed to their familiars.

Catherine Parsons, a Horseheath woman with a good knowledge of witchcraft, published an interesting article in the *Cambridgeshire Antiquarian Society's Proceedings* Vol XIX dated 1st February 1915. At that time witchcraft was by no means a lost art in this village which lies close to the border of Cambridgeshire and Suffolk. 'In this parish we have ghosts as real as ever they were, superstition is rife, the wise woman is fresh in our memory, we have our folklore, certain interesting customs, and cures for almost every ill.'

She speaks of local imps belonging to Mother Redcap, who collected them from her dying sister whose bedroom was filled with the stench of sulphur drifting from her orifices! They were placed 'in a box under which the new owner sat during the journey. Although securely corded no one was allowed to touch it, not even in assisting to lift the box in or out of the cart, for imps are curious creatures and no cords or even iron bars can keep them in bounds unless they are solely under the control of their owner.'

The names of these creatures which resembled white mice were thought to be Bonnie, Blue Cap, Red Cap, Jupiter and Venus. Mother Redcap sent them scuttling down people's chimneys to report back anything which might be of interest to a witch. One was seen sitting on the top of a salt box in Mrs X's chimney corner. It had strange eyes which grew larger then smaller. 'What one does not choose to tell, can always be discovered by the parish witch or wizard with the aid of an imp,' says Miss Parsons.

One day the rag and bone man was stopped by Mother Redcap who demanded to know where he was going. He told her to mind her own business and went on his way, but soon heard something running along the hedge. It was an imp sent to spy on him. He chased it back, but the faster he ran, the faster it ran until it reached its owner and dove between her breasts.

By tradition neither a witch nor a wizard could die until their almost indestructible familiars were either dead themselves or fostered out. One old Fen woman was lingering between life and death and placed hers in the hot bread oven where they cried pitifully like newborn babies, but she was unmoved and when all were silent she too died. The Horseheath witch was buried in 1926, but what happened to Bonnie, Blue Cap, Red Cap, Jupiter and Venus remains a mystery.

HUNTINGDON

The Phantom of the Sapley Treacle Mines

'Treacle mines' are simple bits of foolery or credulity tests for the innocent, rather like 'sky hooks' and 'pigeons' milk'. There have been at least two of these spurious mines in Cambridgeshire. One was at Fen Ditton Docks and the other at the top of Sapley Hill two miles north of Huntingdon town centre, now landmarked by the water tower and the Tesco Superstore. Both have been 'decommissioned', but presumably not that long ago, for they are still remembered.

Before the 1950s when the first phase of the large adjacent industrial estate was commenced, the lonely tree-lined Sapley Mines enjoyed a sinister reputation. Children were especially scared of walking there at night, when the 'treacle phantom' could appear at any time dressed in highwayman's clothes, seated astride a black horse, waiting to murder innocent wayfarers.

This awesome spectre was reputed to be Christopher Ewings, the youngest son of Widow Gatwood, landlady of the Red Lion at Royston. A notorious highway robber, he was finally caught when attempting to rob the mail boy travelling along the Great North Road. Although hanged at Caxton Gibbet in 1673, his spirit broke free to roam the invisible sticky workings at the top of Sapley Hill, which later became a building developer's dream with a traffic system far more frightening than any sticky ghost!

The Phantom Nun

Oliver Cromwell's great-grandfather, Sir Richard Cromwell, built Hinchingbrooke House around the remains of a Benedictine nunnery. This fine residence is now a school. Before the introduction of the new traffic system Nuns Bridge, an ancient many-arched bridge lying alongside its grounds, carried the traffic bound for the A1. At this point the old road is now used as a layby leading off the A604.

A long time ago a young monk and nun often used this bridge to tryst along the beautiful Alconbury Brook. One day they were discovered and punished by death. From time to time the ghostly figure of a young woman dressed in a nun's habit is still claimed to be seen crossing the bridge, although not with her lover but usually another woman.

THE ISLE OF ELY

Johnny and His Female

Johnny the peat cutter lived at the end of the 19th century at Methwold Fen, in a tumble-down hovel just over the Norfolk border. He was a familiar sight in the Isle of Ely, pushing his cart piled high with peat turf and unable to resist every public house en route.

He was an eccentric chap and strongly averse to two things. His water supply and females! Like most local people living in isolated locations, his water came straight from a dyke, which was stained brown from the peat. Believing that it would turn his innards the same colour, he would only drink beer and had an unquenchable thirst. He also refused to wash either himself or his clothes for fear of similar contamination so his skin was covered with a rich patina of filth and he stank to high heaven.

As for females, his now dead mother had been a domineering sort who had compelled him to leave home and rent a few acres of lonely fen. However, people were always telling him that a good female really would make all the difference to his life, but he could not see how. Then late one winter's afternoon he was returning home from his deliveries, with money in his pocket and a gallon jar of beer in his cart, for there is nothing like cold weather to improve the fortunes of a peat cutter. When he reached his door he heard pitiful cries and found an abandoned baby female, half dead with cold.

He took her indoors, wrapped her gently in a blanket, lit the fire and wondered what to do. She was obviously in need of a drink, but probably not alcohol! He called upon the farmer's wife who almost fainted when asked for milk! When told of the abandoned youngster, she reckoned she must have been left by the tinkers who had moved off the Fen that morning and wondered how a mother could be so unloving. Then looking her neighbour straight in the eyes she said that perhaps this was the Almighty's doing, for had not everyone been telling him for ages that a female would make all the difference to his life. If nobody wanted her he should bring her up, for she would be company and could help him when she was older.

The peat cutter took the milk and by the time he reached his hovel was half hoping the little one would not be claimed. She was not, and he called her Jenny. Johnny loved his Jenny and looked after her well, even if he did soon wean her off milk and on to beer. But she thrived and loved her old man. In time it was a bit of a squash for the two of them in the old shack, but who was complaining? Not Jenny. Not Johnny!

When old enough she helped him on his peat rounds and they would stop off at every pub for a pint of beer for him and a half for her. At first people disapproved, but it seemed to do her no harm except when she saw a policeman. For some reason, which Jenny was unable to explain, she always kicked against the law, which the Fen people said proved her link with the tinkers.

The couple were inseparable. They worked well together and Johnny had to admit, a good female did make all the difference, especially one who liked her beer and never washed! Ironically, water was their undoing. One day they were going home, both as drunk as lords, and when crossing the bridge close to their shack, the cart tumbled over the side and they both drowned. They were laid out side by side and people came for miles around to pay their last respects, for Johnny had been a good sort and she one of the best. However, if the truth were told I think it was really Jenny whom they came to see, for a more well-beloved and dissipated donkey would be hard to find!

LITTLEPORT

The Black Dog of Red Mere

Most of the trackways which crossed the old Fens have now disappeared, but Friars Way and Friars Place in Littleport form part of an ancient route used by pilgrims travelling between Thorney Abbey near Peterborough and the holy shrine at Walsingham. Most of the pilgrims were hated by the Fen people, who did not welcome strangers to their land. It is said that some of these men sexually assaulted the local women and a number of these wayfarers never reached their destination, but ended up in the rivers with their throats slit.

To the east of the town and down the minor way leading to Little Ouse off the road to Shippea Hill railway station, is the former Bulldog Bridge, now White House Bridge. The surrounding rich peat fen once lay submerged under reddish coloured stagnant water and was called Red Mere. At that time it was customary for people to preserve mutton for the winter by hanging the carcase tied with mint up the chimney to smoke. The best mint for miles about grew around the edge of the lonely Red Mere.

One summer morning the lady of the manor of Littleport asked a pretty young servant girl to gather as much of the herb as she could carry in her apron. She set off early in the morning, but soon the sun was beating down and by the time she reached the treeless, strangely coloured marsh, the heat was intolerable. The girl picked the mint and headed for home, but as she approached Bulldog Bridge she could go no further without resting. She fell asleep alongside the trackway, but was soon awoken by a large, sweating friar tugging at her skirt. Fighting for her honour and screaming for help, she put up a good fight, but there was no one about on that boiling hot day. The pilgrim pinned her down and holding a knife to her throat, threatened to use it if she did not surrender to him.

The terrified virgin prayed for help and immediately an enormous snarling dog jumped out of the reeds. It sprang upon her assailant and sank its great fangs into his flesh as the girl fell into a dead faint. When consciousness returned she saw her attacker, now at the point of death, plunge his blade into the dog's ribs. Whining pitifully, the animal crawled alongside her and died in her arms.

She ran back to Littleport, still with her apron filled with mint, and told her story. That night a gang of men went to Red Mere to dispose of the friar's body in the bloody mere and they buried the dog by the side of the track, close to where the present bridge crosses White House Drain. Its bones may still be there, for they say that if you go to this place at sunset on a summer evening, you too may see the ghostly Black Dog of Red Mere walking up and down the road before disappearing into thin air.

MADINGLEY

Lady Ursula's Ghost

Madingley Hall is a large Tudor mansion owned by Cambridge University. It is reputed to be haunted by Lady Ursula, the wife of Sir John Hynde who began its construction in circa 1543. He died in 1550, leaving the task of completing the building works to his son and heir, Sir Francis Hynde. Materials were taken from St Etheldreda's church at Histon, which he demolished for the purpose. Its fine hammer-beam roof was incorporated in the Hall's turret attic, old timbers, lead and even the font all had their use with the surplus sold off to the highest bidders. The devout Lady Ursula was so angered by her son's sacrilegious behaviour that she went into a decline and died. Although the Norman font was eventually removed to Madingley parish church, her ghost continued to walk the Hall and its grounds, wringing its hands in despair.

Charles I took refuge here when escaping from the Parliamentarians after hiding at Childerley Manor nearby. Madingley was then owned by the Royalist Sir John Coton, who welcomed the King when he arrived unannounced at midnight disguised as a peasant and gave him shelter in a small chamber. This was to be dubbed 'The Dog Room', for supposedly it was a barking dog which eventually betrayed the monarch to the enemy when they scoured the place in search of him.

69

MARCH

A Railway Story

March was once an important railway town, but successive financial cutbacks have reduced it to a shadow of its former glory. It is now better known for the high-risk prison built on part of the old 68 acre marshalling yards at Whitemoor. However, in the past, after the destruction of the Hamm marshalling yards in Germany during the Second World War, this was the largest rail freight complex in Europe. During one day in August 1942 it handled 59 trains, pulling 3,841 wagons, and by 1953 the overall capacity of the yards had reached 7,000 wagons in 24 hours.

A little after midnight on 2nd June 1944 driver Mr Ben Gimbert, fireman Mr Nightall and guard Mr Herbert Clarke took an ammunition train from Whitemoor bound for Earl's Colne, near Colchester, carrying 50 wagons packed with bombs. As they made their way across the Fens and were approaching Soham station, the driver saw to his horror that the front wagon containing forty 500 lb bombs was on fire.

He was able to stop the train 90 yards from the station, and he and his crew managed to free the red hot couplings and push the wagon into a siding. The bombs in the uncoupled wagon exploded as they passed through the station, killing the fireman and a signalman, but the accident would have been far worse had the front wagon not been isolated. Ben Gimbert was badly injured, but despite being thrown 80 feet in the air and badly concussed, Herbert Clarke staggered more than two miles back down the track, laying detonators to warn any approaching trains, before collapsing.

Although the station and some 700 houses were badly damaged, the brave action of these three men had prevented an even worse explosion and certain loss of life. The names of Messrs Gimbert, Nightall and Clarke were added to the long list of wartime heroes who played their part at home.

MEPAL

Ann Bentley's Fright

At the time of her sister Maria Salmons' death in the 1840s, Ann Bentley was living at Mepal, a small Fen village near Ely. She took her two motherless nephews to live with her and, as later told to a reporter from the *Cambridge Chronicle*, this was the start of her troubles. About a week after the funeral she was woken by the sound of footsteps shuffling around her bed and it felt as if the youngest child sleeping by her side was being pulled away by a strong force. With difficulty she lit a candle, and saw clearly her dead sister standing in the doorway, looking exactly as she had done in life, dressed in her usual cotton dress and cap.

The two faced each other and the spectre then raised its hands in the air and kept asking, 'How's Harry, Ann, how's Harry?' (unfortunately the article fails to give the identity of 'Harry', presumably one of her sons).

'Very poorly,' Ann said, ending their brief conversation.

After a while the figure walked into the next room where the eldest child slept. Ann followed and found the boy out of bed, standing trance-like by the

71

window. The ghost stared at him but made no contact, then disappeared still muttering, 'Harry! Harry!'

Over the next two weeks Maria Salmons made her nightly visitations, but did not speak. The terrified Ann Bentley believed she was trying to make contact with her children and begged the priest to rid them of this apparition. After much persuasion he agreed to conduct an exorcism, which took place one night with Ann, her father, mother and a neighbour in attendance, all waiting anxiously by candlelight for the undead to appear. At about 8 pm footsteps were heard and Maria appeared in the doorway, listening intently to the priest's ineffective service.

'What is your trouble?' he asked the relentless phantom.

'I will come as long as I can come,' was its enigmatic reply.

These encounters lasted for some two and a half years, until Maria's widower John remarried and took their children to live with him and his wife in their new cottage. Ann never saw the ghost again, for it transferred its attention to Mr and Mrs Salmons and often pulled the children from their beds. She described these hauntings as 'powerful disturbances', adding that John was very afraid to go out to the stables after dark unless one of his boys went with him, for Maria often appeared to him there.

This troubled marriage lasted 15 years, until both husband and wife died within a few months of each other. With her children now fully grown, Maria finally rested quietly in her grave.

OLD WESTON

The Frightening of Molly Gresham

About 130 years ago Molly Gresham lived with her widowed brother Tom at 'The Cottage', which stands on a rise at the junction of the main road with the church road. This hard working couple got on well together, she the perfect spinster housekeeper, he the uncomplaining farmhand and provider. However, tragedy was about to strike which would affect Molly forever.

One morning after visiting friends and staying out too long, she hurried up the road to get Tom's dinner on the table by noon. It being elevated, she had a good view of her home from some distance and noticed a man standing by the front door. Not expecting visitors she wondered who he could be. Certainly not her brother or a regular caller, for in those days most people reserved this entrance for important occasions only. Many still do. There is an unwritten rule in much of rural Cambridgeshire: friends go round the back, sales people and religious callers stick to the front where they can be ignored.

So Molly had time to puzzle over this black-dressed stranger standing as still as a statue outside her cottage. When she reached the gate he offered no acknowledgement of her greeting. Now feeling very apprehensive she demanded to know his business. Still refusing to speak he stared with eyes which bored straight through her, then floated up in the air, hovered above the hedge for some time, then evaporated!

Molly stood rooted to the spot. Had she just seen a ghost? What should she tell Tom? However, in her simple life there was a time for cooking dinner and a time for being frightened, so she went indoors to give herself a few minutes' peace and quiet before peeling the potatoes. Then a sense of foreboding flooded through her. Something was wrong with Tom! She hurried along the passageway and there he was, the brother who had never suffered a day's illness, lying dead upon the parlour floor.

Her story told to the authorities concerning the unwelcome caller was confirmed by a woman living in the now derelict cottages situated on the main road, who had been cleaning windows at the time. She too had seen the weird stranger across the way, the sight of whom had made her faint.

Although the coroner's inquest recorded death by natural causes, Molly was not convinced, remaining adamant that the floating stranger was a harbinger of death who had called for her Tom. The experience turned her into a local oddity, for there is often the suspicion, especially in close knit communities, that those connected with the supernatural become entangled in its power. Eyes peered from behind curtains, tongues rattled and fingers wagged as the gossips in Old Weston had much to report after the frightening of Molly Gresham.

ORTON LONGUEVILLE

Raveley Jack

A village once occupied by the Romans, Orton Longueville is now part of Greater Peterborough. It leads down to the river Nene, where a gravel shallow is said to deepen into what was once called 'Raveley's Hole'.

Sometime between 1840 and 1850 a ragged, lanky youth aged about 16 years walked into Peterborough. As he did not know his whereabouts let alone his own name, the locals dubbed him 'Jack', and gave him the surname 'Raveley' after the little Huntingdonshire village which may have been his home. Better known as 'Raveley Jack', the stranger soon settled into his new environment, where his eccentricities made him the joke of the city and constant tease of the young.

Their question, 'Jack, why are you so daft?', always received the same reply. It was because one day he got too close to the town mill, and one of its sails had hit him on the head. To his taunters this only confirmed his stupidity, for surely anyone with half a wit would have steered clear of its sweep. However, what Jack lacked in the head was gained in his feet, for he was an incredible runner and was always winning races.

At that time the superstitious heeded the old Peterborough adage:

'If in the Minster Close a hare
Should for itself have made a lair,
Be sure before the week is down
A fire will rage within the town.'

and of course the day came when one appeared in this holy quarter. Before the local sportsmen could reach for their guns, Jack was off chasing the frightened creature over tombstones, through bushes, first in one corner, then another, up and down, round and round, all the while whooping, screaming and waving his hat. Soon a large excited crowd had converged around the cathedral, all agreeing that this simpleton had more poke in him than a greyhound! They egged him on as hour after hour he pursued his quarry around the lush pastures of Minster Close. Eventually the hare dropped to the ground with exhaustion, but there were several miles left in Jack, who wrung its neck and paraded his trophy around the city to loud cheers and trumpet blasts.

Despite his tattered appearance, this innocent paid good attention to his personal hygiene and in the summer took frequent bathes in the river Nene. One day he visited the gravel shallow at Orton Longueville and although unable to swim, waded across to the opposite meadow.

Sadly, like much about him, his sense of direction was none too bright. On the return journey he lost his way, tripped and plunged headlong into the deep hole where he drowned. His remains were buried in a pauper's grave in Woodston churchyard, but his fame lived on. For a long time this part of the Nene was called 'Raveley's Hole', in memory of the lad who chased a hare around the Minster Close and, if there were truth in the old rhyme, may have saved Peterborough from the ravages of fire!

OXLODE

The Rich Fool

This tiny hamlet shelters against the Hundred Foot Drain close to Ely. Its only approach is down a very long bumpy track and it is easily passed by. This is where the legendary John Leaford is reputed to have lived towards the end of the 17th century. He started out as a navvy maintaining the river banks and dykes, living in a crude hut made of turf and thatched with sedge. By now the 'Fen Tigers' who had fought so vigorously to halt the drainage undertaking had long thrown in the towel, some even purchasing the new reclaimed land wrung from bog and swamp.

However, this great engineering scheme devised by the Dutchman Cornelius Vermuyden was flawed and both he and his financial backers or 'Adventurers' of the 17th century would have faced bankruptcy had Charles II not bailed them out. The levels of the main drainage channels were calculated incorrectly, thereby preventing a swift flow of water out to sea. They silted up, making them higher than the land dykes, which now required their water to be raised to the higher levels by pumps powered by the wind.

By the time of this cautionary tale the Fens and its people remained vulnerable to extreme weather, with much of the new land still only fit for summer grazing. Water was a constant threat to life and livelihood. There are numerous accounts of dreadful inundations, for this region needed and still needs manpower, banks, sluice gates and pumps to keep it dry. Floodwater has always been a bugbear, the stuff of nightmares and folklore.

When not working on the drains, John Leaford went fishing and wildfowling. He was a skilled sportsman who sold his catch and saved hard. He bought a parcel of new land and life looked promising. There followed several years of perfect weather. He extended his boundaries, exploited his workers and eventually built a fine mansion beside the river bank, not far from his simple hut which was left abandoned. Money begets money, so Leaford married a beautiful rich woman, whilst his arrogance continued to keep pace with his prosperity. His workers were polite enough to his face, but behind his back called him 'The Rich Fool', not without reason.

As a landowner he was responsible for the maintenance of the waterways lying on his property, but ignored the obligation, saying there were better things to do with his men and money. Despite numerous dire warnings he forbad his labourers to attempt any of the necessary work. Time passed, the seasons yielded good harvests with his riches increasing beyond belief, until a severe winter made its mark. The snow lay deep for several weeks, but miraculously its melt was contained by the drainage system. Leaford was jubilant, he was right not to have wasted his money!

This was followed by seven days and seven nights of continuous rain. The flood water poured down from the uplands into the already swollen and clogged up man-made channels, whose banks on Leaford's land groaned with pressure. He quickly changed his mind, ordering his men to repair their foundations and strengthen the ramparts, but it was too late, their efforts were in vain. The Hundred Foot Drain was breached, totally destroying his farm and much of the surrounding Bedford Level. For as far as the eye could see there was nothing but water littered with the debris of buildings, straw stacks and the bloated corpses of humans and animals.

Although his great mansion had been the first to fall, by a strange quirk of fate John Leaford's tiny hut had withstood the inundation. The now disgraced and broken man who had lost everything including his family, returned to his humble beginnings where his name was cursed for many years. They say the Rich Fool's greed had put back the land reclamation programme for more than a lifetime.

PETERBOROUGH

The Ethereal Choir

Although the Romans occupied a legionary fort at Longthorpe, it was during the Saxon era that Peterborough, then called Medeshamstede, took shape around the church founded in AD 655 by King Paeda, the first Christian king of Mercia. This was sacked by Danish invaders in AD 870, rebuilt some 100 years later as a Benedictine monastery, then damaged in 1069 in the last efforts of the Fen hero, Hereward the Wake, to resist the Norman conquest.

The present glorious structure, which was started in 1118 by Abbot John de Sais, holds incredible memories for Trevor Bevis, a local historian and author. Now retired, he used to work in the printing trade in Peterborough and often walked into town during his lunch break to eat his sandwiches within the shelter of the cathedral cloisters. Afterwards he would spend some peaceful moments inside this fine Norman building which he loves so much, savouring the tranquillity far removed from the clatter and bang of industry.

One particularly drab grey day during November 1958, the sort most associated with the Fens, he entered the cathedral through the side door, noticing his friend the senior verger working at the west end. Trevor had his customary warm against a large Victorian stove, then wandered off towards the choir. It was unusually quiet, in fact apart from the verger quietly going about his business, he appeared to have the place to himself. But this was not so! For suddenly there came the faint sound of chanting voices drifting his way. Believing it was choir practice, which was strange because the choristers usually rehearsed away from the cathedral, he went to enjoy the unexpected bonus, but their stalls were empty. He stood alone listening to the most beautiful sound of vespers sung in Latin.

'The unaccompanied voices became clearer,' he recalls, 'and they changed with impressive precision, hitting exactly the right notes with commendable metre, lilting up and down in complete unison. Thoroughly absorbed, I stood rooted to the spot and turned my head for better effect to catch the sound which occasionally seemed muted as though a thin wall existed between the ethereal voices and me.

'Then it happened. All around, the unseen choir seemed to occupy their old places in the stalls, and I was in the middle of it all. If I had reached out I felt I could have touched the monks. I knew they were there. It was as if they had approached in procession ... it was as if they were singing for me.'

Although aware of his immediate surroundings, he had the sensation of standing on air in some blissful other dimension, his flesh tingling as if touched by some great spiritual force. This marvel lasted for about seven minutes, when the chanting ceased and with reluctance the listener came back to earth and made his way back down the nave. The building was still empty, except for the verger who asked what he had been doing in the choir, for he had noticed his head turning from side to side, as if keeping time with some rhythm.

Upon hearing this story the verger confided that over the last 20 years to his knowledge at least two other visitors had heard similar chanting coming from an invisible choir. Although he has returned many times since that amazing day, Trevor Bevis has never again heard the spectral choir, but remains thankful for those few wonderful moments spent in this enigmatic cathedral.

RAMSEY

Two Tooth Pullers and a Ghost

Rowland Lavender, better known by his nickname 'British' or 'Brit' for short, was 88 years old in 1991 when Bill Bedford, a founder member of the Ramsey Rural Life Museum, tape recorded his memories. Their friendship spanned 65 years, and for 55 of them Brit was employed on the de Ramsey estate, turning his hand to anything that required attention, from hedge laying to boot cleaning. Over several weeks these two gentle people sat by the fire swapping stories, sometimes breaking the pattern to sing a few songs, each delighting in the other's company.

Four years later I listened to those memories by the warmth of my own fire. With a little prompting from his interviewer, Brit described late Saturday nights in the town, when a strange pair of outsiders often turned up after the market traders had packed up and gone home. One was an escapologist who could wriggle free from great swathes of clanking chains and tightly knotted ropes. His companion, who had an insatiable appetite for things best not eaten, swallowed pocket watches which, according to Brit, could be heard ticking inside him.

Of course, it was the withdrawing of the timepiece which provided the best entertainment. He would splutter and cough, wide eyed and red faced, to great cheers and cat calls. 'When it come by that little clack what hangs down in your throat [uvula], that made his eyes water! Then he'd chew up a bit of clay pipe and if anyone wanted any teeth pulling out, these chaps would do it for nothing. They used to have a big drum so that if you hollered no one heard you!' Brit and his friend tutted and laughed nervously.

And speaking of pain – Mr Oliver G. Howe, whose chemist shop stood on the corner of Great Whyte and the High Street, could not go unmentioned by Brit, for like most dentists at that time he extracted teeth without anaesthetic.

'You never said, "Could you pull a tooth out for me, Mr Howe?" because he could! Yes, once he got a hold on it, he never let go on it until it come out! He'd sit you in an ordinary armchair, then he'd go to the front door and lock it, then he'd go to the back and put the bolt on that one too. Then he'd ask you, "Open your mouth, which one is it?" And he'd come round with them forceps an' tap the one what had been aching so as to make you jump. His forceps were very near as big as pig ringers, with a grip on the handle like these here wire cutters do. After the job it was, "How much Mr Howe?" He always charged a shilling and when he opened the door you were out of there like a greyhound out of a trap. Out on that road you were! You didn't wait for him to ask you to go. You used to get out as quick as you could. He was cruel!'

And so the conversation continued. It made me think of other Ramsey stories. Although Brit did not mention the dilapidated Biggin Lane Maltings which were demolished in 1943 when the adjoining RAF Upwood extended its airfield, he more than likely joined the others when they strapped their Fen Runner skates to their boots and sped around its moat when the weather was right. The lone building stood somewhat eerily on top of a gentle hill on the Bury side of town, but the only hint of its existence now is the clump of elm trees standing close to the trackway leading down this rise.

According to folklore Biggin Lane, now a prime housing development, used to be a daunting place, being located so close to these reputedly haunted maltings, once the property of Ramsey Abbey. The monks brewed their 'exceptionally strong liquor' here and the apparition of a distressed young woman was claimed to be seen on occasion drifting in and out of its stone walls. Sadly the spectre has no folkloric history, but similar ghostly young maidens who haunt abbey maltings are usually believed to have been ravished then murdered by intoxicated monks.

Certainly, given the right hour and weather conditions, this crumbling building perched on the highest point of the horizon must have looked very foreboding, but was it any more frightening than Brit's legends in the making? Which would have scared you most? The anticipation of a spectre materialising in the middle of nowhere or the sight of a flesh and blood man who has just eaten a clay pipe and regurgitated your watch, transforming himself into a voluntary tooth-smith, whilst his weird friend burst out of bondage to bang a drum which will mask your screams? And are these two prospects any more terrifying than the sound of that determined dentist, Mr Oliver G. Howe, bolting his back and front doors before giving you a shilling's worth of pain? Which would have made the biggest imprint on your mind and made it a story worth telling?

ST IVES

The Legend of All Saints' Church

The graceful spire of this mostly 15th century church is not original. The first crashed to the ground during a hurricane in 1741 and its replacement needed repairing when an aeroplane crashed into it. As if this were not enough, its bells are reputed to be bewitched!

It happened a long time ago, late one night in July when the parishioners were awoken by a single bell clanging eerily through their dreams. Befuddled men and women tumbled from their beds, hurrying to the church to stop whoever it was from disturbing their peace at that ungodly hour. The bell continued to ring as each door was tried in turn, always proving to be securely barred. The key to the main entrance was located and when the lock turned the bell immediately fell silent. This sudden hush was said to be more frightening than the raucous boom from above.

A brave few rushed to investigate the mystery, pushing and jostling their way up the narrow stairs to the belfry, where one bell rope swung as if just pulled, but with no sign of its ringer. A thorough search of the church and its roof provided no clues. The ensuing impromptu conference held in the graveyard concluded with the citizens of St Ives declaring the bells to be bewitched and that they should be condemned to silence for evermore.

Their priest Father Augustine dismissed this decision, confident that his ringers would not let the bells fall silent. However, the next call to matins and vespers was unannounced and remained so throughout the week. The following Sabbath was equally soundless, but on the next he preached a stern sermon from the pulpit, railing against the foolish gossip which had gripped the town.

'Faith arms us against such things and ye, oh ye of faith, it is because ye have it in so small a portion, that ye are frightened by the accidental clang of a bell, which any natural cause may hereafter explain, from going forward as usual to call us by God's holy bells to His most holy service...'

He was interrupted by a loud voice bellowing from the back of the church ordering him to be silent. 'Who speaks and why?' demanded the priest.

'You speak of faith in others, but have you got it yourself? Will you ring the bewitched bell first?' dared the invisible accuser.

Father Augustine crossed himself and accepted the challenge, adding that such was his faith he would also spend a night in the belfry. 'Then do it!' came the reply.

The priest asked the congregation if this would be proof enough. They gave a low murmur of assent and it was agreed this would take place the following night.

News spread further than neighbouring Huntingdon and sightseers made their way to St Ives, some travelling great distances on foot, by horse and in laden boats which moored along the river Ouse between the osiers and the river bank. Hundreds gathered in the churchyard after vespers, all thrilled and silenced by the sight of Father Augustine stepping slowly out upon the church roof from a stone window. He faced the multitude of upturned faces tinged red in the setting sun.

'My friends,' he called. 'See me. I am not afraid. God himself will shelter me under his holy bells.' He raised his hands in an unspoken blessing and entered the tower.

In time darkness emptied the churchyard of people. Then at midnight the death bell rang. Solemn and deep it penetrated the stillness of St Ives, forcing disturbed sleepers from their beds to All Saints' church. As before, the unlocking of the door silenced the bell, but this time none dared climb the stairs to determine the fate of the priest who did not answer their calls. They waited until daybreak to explore the tower. Father Augustine was found dead beneath the bewitched bells, the cause remaining a mystery, as did the inopportune chiming which ceased from that night.

ST NEOTS

The Ghost of the New Inn

Parliamentary forces were billeted at the New Inn, then a posting house, prior to their storming Kimbolton Castle during the Civil War. Although much of the building was reconstructed in 1908, the bar is said to be haunted. The first sighting appears to have occurred in 1963 when the landlady Mrs Kerr, who had trouble sleeping, went down to the empty bar to make herself, of all things, a cup of coffee. Suddenly the apparition of a tall slender man dressed in a long cloak drifted across the room and out through a bolted door leading to the yard, where it vanished without trace. She was to encounter the spectre on several occasions. From time to time other people claim to have experienced a sense of unease in the very spot where this unidentifiable and now invisible ghost first scared Mrs Kerr.

The Psychic Smell at the Royal Oak

The present hotel standing in the High Street was mainly rebuilt in 1885 to replace a much smaller structure, but has not escaped the all too familiar paranormal fate of so many public houses. The building had been exorcised before Mr and Mrs Hart took over the tenancy in the early 1960s, but unbeknown to them its old ways were returning. Out of the blue and without natural cause, Mr Hart started to smell most dreadfully each time he entered the old part of the building, the stench falling from him when he left. The poor odoriferous chap was affecting trade, so a team of psychic investigators were invited to hold a seance in the public bar to get to the bottom of the mystery.

Using special equipment, they declared the source of the spectral smell to be a man who had committed suicide in that quarter of the inn by hanging himself from a meat hook. His body had remained undiscovered for several days, hence the haunting took the form of a reek of putrid flesh which was attaching itself to the landlord. After another exorcism Mr Hart was nothing but fragrant.

Uncle Peter and 'One-Armed' Squire

During the 19th century two members of the large Squire family lived in houses both facing Walnut Tree Square off Brook Street. James, better known as 'One Armed' due to his deformity, was perpetually at war with his neighbouring uncle Peter, who was the son of the swarthy faced James 'Old Mahogany' Squire, so called because of his complexion. These men argued over everything and nothing in particular, especially the ownership of the walnut tree which gave its name to the square. After years of bitter feuding Peter chopped it down one night in blind temper and so the hatred continued.

One Armed's boundary fence was protected from damage by carriage wheels by a huge boulder weighing several hundredweight. In 1883 the *St Neots Chronicle* reported that someone had stolen it and thrown it into the brook. Mr Squire offered a reward of £2 to discover the persons responsible, but the culprit – or because of its weight, the culprits – was never found.

The stone was restored to its rightful position, but after the owner's death was taken to the yard of the Royal Oak posting house in the High Street, to be used as a mounting block. It now stands on the grass verge of the Little Barford road to mark the urban district council boundary and, for those who know the story, to remind them of the acrimonious Peter Squire and his equally aggressive one-armed nephew.

SOHAM

Granny's Rapid Motion Pills

Little Dot was born at Soham near Ely towards the end of the 19th century. They called him 'Little Dot' because he was so tiny, and his proper name is long forgotten. He grew, if that is the right word, into a con man and looked the part with his secondhand suit of clothing with huge trouser hems, spats, walking cane and well greased hair. When his dubious career was temporarily halted by a prison sentence most said 'good riddance', with his widowed mother echoing the sentiment.

He was more or less forgotten until a couple of years later when a local farmer was visiting Cambridge market and heard an all too familiar voice. With his hand guarding his money pocket he joined the large crowd gathered around Little Dot, who was selling laxatives, insisting that constipation lay at the root of all political and personal evil. Cure this and you would live if not forever, then at least for a very long time, in a world brimming with prosperity and contentment. However, this Utopia could only be gained from taking the correct dosage of what he considered to be the finest laxative in the world – which he called his 'Granny's Rapid Motion Pills'. These he made personally from a recipe copied from the old lady's pocket book, she having died the week before at the age of 98, not from natural causes but following a speed skating accident in a race which she was set to win!

'Now, ladies and gentleman,' he continued, 'I am not offering you my Granny's Rapid Motion Pills for one shilling a box. I am not offering them to you for ninepence, nor am I offering them for sixpence. No, my friends, I am here to help, so all I am asking is just threepence a box. Just threepence a box to cure all the evils of this world and for you to stay healthy for ever! And as an English gentleman, my word is my bond. Take one pill and if it doesn't work take two and if they don't work take eight and if they're no good come back next week and I will pay you five shillings a week for the rest of your life! Yes, ladies and gentlemen, five shillings a week for the rest of your life and I can't say fairer than that!'

The gullible parted with their money and Dot departed from their company and did another stretch in prison. Then, being good with words he turned to religion and became a missionary going around East Anglia preaching hellfire and damnation, which always produced heavy collection boxes from repentant sinners. His congregations watched with relish as he got more and more steamed up over the evils of drink, gambling and especially fallen women, who were his obsession. Little Dot's face would turn bright red as he jumped up and down, waving his arms, shouting and screaming in high pitched tones laced with the smell of whisky.

One of his most memorable sermons was preached in the chapel at Soham Fen, where with hindsight he should have heeded the warning regarding a prophet being without honour in his own country. An extraordinarily long queue had formed long before the doors were opened in anticipation of a good night's entertainment.

Some three quarters of an hour into the service the diminutive preacher climbed the pulpit steps and elevated himself to a sensible height on his hidden soapbox. With his chin just above the carved oak rail, he waved his hands in the style of an unleashed windmill in a Fen blow. 'Fire! Fire!' he screamed and the happy onlookers knew their Little Dot would not let them down.

He filled his lungs and screamed:
'At night the cry of fire rang out,
Are they all saved came the fireman's shout!'
before vanishing from view, which was not uncommon for over-exertion usually made him fall off his perch. He popped up unharmed and spoke of his missionary travels around Eastern England. He raged about the iniquities of Ipswich and the evils of Norwich. Next it was the turn of Cambridge, a satanical place of learning with empty churches, full taverns, starving children and prosperous whores. So many whores! You could not move for fallen women in this city, which was no better than Sodom and Gomorrah. It stank of Hell and all were deaf to his words!

'Then I came to Ely and reminded the harlots and painted strumpets to consider Lot's wife, but they knew her not.' Stifled laughter filled the small chapel as their man proceeded to take them on a diabolical tour which terminated at the gates of Hell and the fiery furnace. His assurance that this place could be avoided upon the receipt of generous donations to his mission was greeted with scepticism.

90

Little Dot was obviously leading up to the grand finale. He picked up the Good Book, held it above his head and leaning over at an extremely dangerous angle for one so finely balanced, bellowed out, 'Consider the sins of the world! Consider the women of pleasure who tempt innocent men with their foul bodies, consider the evils of the demon drink! Oh my good people, in your hearts you know the cure for these iniquities.' Once more he thumped the Good Book and implored, 'For God's sake – tell me – what is the cure?'

And the farmer who had seen him at Cambridge market shouted back, 'Why don't you take one of your Granny's Rapid Motion Pills, Dot, and if that don't do the trick, you take two and if they don't work swallow the ****** boxful, then come back next week and we'll pay you five bob a week for the rest of your life!'

There was a loud crash as the preacher fell from grace and the chapel erupted with laughter, so ending what was to become a popular Fen story.

SOHAM MERE

King Canute and the Brave Pudding

Soham Mere is now fertile arable land, but before its reclamation was a wet area some ten miles in radius, lying in a hollow to the south of Soham village. Canute, the Danish King of England (c994–1035), came one year to visit the monks of Ely in time for Candlemas Day, 2nd February. The Fens were frozen over and his men refused to travel further lest the ice break and their monarch drown. However, being a good and pious man the King exclaimed, 'Hold ice or break ice, I will keep the Feast of the Purification with the good monks of Ely. And be there one bold Fenner that will go before over the ice by Soham Mere and show the way, I will be the next to follow!'

None immediately came forward, but living close to this treacherous expanse of swamp and water which claimed many lives in fog and frost, was one named Brithmer. He was better known from his exceeding fatness as 'Budde', or 'Pudding'. It was he who offered to go before the King and show him the safe way across the frozen waste.

Canute, who though stout of nature was slight of build exclaimed, 'If the ice can bear thy weight, it can well bear mine! Walk on and I shall follow!' So Pudding made his way across the bending, cracking ice whilst his majesty followed at a convenient distance, following by his courtiers. Despite a few minor mishaps they reached Ely unscathed, even if half dead with cold. To reward this good deed Canute relinquished his guide's serfdom and gave him several acres of dry pasture, with milch cows and flocks of sheep. This now prosperous Fenner or Fenman was called 'Master Brithmer' instead of 'Fat Pudding', and treated with respect by the cowards who would have had their king turn back from Ely.

STAPLEFORD

The Gog Magog Hills

Two giants, Gog and Magog, reputedly the last of a race of giants destroyed by Brutus, the legendary founder of Britain, are said to be buried here and until the beginning of the 18th century a huge figure could be seen cut into these hills.

The Iron Age Wandlebury Fort lies at the summit. According to legend if a warrior dared enter it in the moonlight and cried, 'Knight to knight, come forth,' a ghostly night-rider would appear from nowhere and do battle with him. Although his companions could watch from behind the entrenchments, only the knight could enter the camp.

In the Middle Ages a young knight named Sir Osbert who possessed every noble and daring quality visited a wealthy Cambridge merchant, who held a feast in his honour. Afterwards the assembly gathered round the fire exchanging stories, when someone from these parts told the old tale. Sir Osbert asked if it were true, but as none could say for certain he decided to put it to the test. Dressed in complete armour and accompanied by his squire he set off on his quest, their horses' iron-shod hooves sparking on the cobble stones as they galloped out into the countryside, bound for the moonlit hills.

Upon reaching their destination Sir Osbert ordered his man to remain outside the perimeter of the fort whilst he steered his mount through the small opening and cried, 'Knight to knight, come forth!' Immediately there appeared a huge supernatural knight seated astride a great jet black horse. He closed the vizor of his black helmet and with his lance drawn level came thundering towards his mortal opponent. Although no words were exchanged, many blows were dealt until at last Sir Osbert knocked the night-rider to the ground. According to the laws of chivalry he was now entitled to the loser's horse as the spoils of conquest. Furious that his steed was being captured, the night-rider threw his lance at his adversary then vanished without trace. The weapon caught Sir

Osbert a glancing blow in the thigh, causing less pain than a bee sting.

Leading his prize by the reins he and his squire rode back to Cambridge where they were greeted by a large crowd eager to learn if the old story was true. When told, they marvelled at his bravery and admired the well deserved reward. Sir Osbert ordered this horse of flesh and blood to be well tethered and watched throughout the night lest it attempt to return to its supernatural master. Now very tired he prepared for bed, but when removing his armour noticed that one of his greaves, or pieces of shin armour, was filled with clotted blood. Only then did he remember his wounded thigh, which a servant was summoned to attend.

All was quiet until daybreak when the black horse reared and pranced like a thing possessed, broke its tethering and galloped off towards the hills. Neither it nor its ghostly master were seen again. Sir Osbert's injury soon healed, but he returned to his home with a perpetual reminder of his Cambridgeshire adventure. Each year on the anniversary the old wound broke open, bled profusely then healed immediately. His story was kept alive in the oral tradition until Gervase of Tilbury included it in his *Otia Imperialia* written in the early 13th century.

There are other stories connected with these hills. Traditionally, a golden chariot lies beneath Copley Hill, a tumulus to the east, whilst a mysterious pagan horse is said to be interred beneath the western beech trees. The story of the latter may have become confused with that of the Godolphin Arabian, one of three horses from which all British racing stock is descended. This famous horse is actually buried in a grave dated 1753, which was situated in the cupola stable block attached to the now demolished Godolphin mansion.

STILTON

Cheese and Ghosts Rub Shoulders at the Bell

The annual Easter Stilton cheese rolling competition is a popular attraction, when teams of four roll wooden 'cheeses' down the main street. Although the name of this old Huntingdonshire village is inextricably linked to the delicious creamy blue-veined cheese, the first of its kind is thought to have been made at 'The Old Manor House' at Wymondham in east Leicestershire, possibly in the 14th century. However, the local connection is authentic. Stilton was one of the most important former staging posts along the Great North Road, now the A1, and became the main trading station for this popular cheese which was first supplied to travellers using the Bell Inn. People enjoyed this speciality and carried far and wide the praises of the excellent 'Stilton cheese'.

This was music to the ears of Cooper Thornhill, who besides being the landlord of the Bell, was a business entrepreneur and the Eastern England corn representative for the bankers Coutts & Co. In the 1740s he personally contracted with Frances and William Pawlett of Wymondham, Leicestershire to market their blue cheese, trading from the Bell. Wagonloads of 'Stilton' were dispatched to his London contacts and although geographically relocated, this favoured commodity was placed firmly on the culinary map.

Mercantile acumen was not his only strength. Thornhill was a celebrated betting man and horse rider. On 29th October 1745 he accepted a wager to ride a distance of 213 miles in 15 hours. Leaving Stilton at 4 am he rode to the King's Arms, Shoreditch, which he reached at 7.50 am, immediately returning home and then setting out once more for London, reaching Shoreditch at 4.15 in the afternoon. He had travelled 213 miles in 12 hours and 15 minutes and won his wager with time to spare. An old chronicler who mentions these facts in a private diary adds, 'many horses engaged.'

He also caused a stir one day when he rode to Kimbolton races on an ordinary mare. Reckoning the entrants to be no better than his mount, he made some rude comments, entered the race without dismounting and returned home with the first prize and trophy!

Although Thornhill died in 1752 and was buried in the local churchyard, he was destined to haunt the Bell, along with three other spectres! Dick Turpin, that ubiquitous highway robber, walks the bedroom in which he hid for eight weeks whilst on the run from the law. Apparently they finally caught up with him, but he managed to leap out of the window straight onto the back of his horse which was waiting patiently below and effect an escape (see also Buckden). This is now called 'Dick's Room', and has been turned into a small lounge adjoining the first floor dining room.

Daniel Defoe, the author and traveller, often stayed at the Bell, especially between 1697 and 1701 when serving as the secret agent to William III of Orange. He made several references to this village in his three volume work, *A Tour through the Whole Island of Great Britain*, published between 1724 and 1726. Therefore it comes as no surprise to learn that his ghost used to sit against the stone fireplace in the present reception area, smoking a clay pipe, dressed in silver buckled shoes and a velvet suit, topped off with a tricorn hat. Just because it has not been seen for some while does not mean it is not there!

Far more chilling is 'The lady' who still materialises in the three bedrooms situated in the oldest part of the building. Sometimes she sits on a bed, leaving an indentation, or paces restlessly up and down the floor. Her footsteps are heard from below, even when these rooms are known to be locked and unoccupied. Guests have also been awoken at night with the eerie sensation that someone has been lying on top of them, but only in the most ancient rooms of this hotel whose magnificent sign spans the pavement.

The Family Skeleton

If the Crewe family had succeeded in slowly torturing Martha to death, this too might have been a ghost story, for given time her shocking tale could easily have spun her into the supernatural. She, Martha Crewe, would have been a thin tortured apparition screaming out in death as so often in life, 'Please, please give me some food and drink.' But mercifully the Grim Reaper was waylaid and in August 1856 her father Edward and two sisters Rebecca and Eliza stood before the Huntingdon magistrates on the charge of attempting to starve her to death.

From the report there is no doubt that the girl's troubles were common knowledge in Stilton. Presumably the villagers soothed their consciences, knowing they had tried to do their best, but were always thwarted by her family or bureaucracy. Those who went to church or chapel probably mentioned her in their prayers, but still her screams rang in their ears. At the end of the day, 19 year old Martha was left to fend for herself, until too weak to stand, she was snatched from the stranglehold of her family from hell.

Susan Smith, a neighbour, said in evidence at the

hearing: 'For the last three years I often heard Martha crying in her father's house for bread. When she came to my house I gave her a slice of bread and ham. Her ghostly look frightened me; I thought it was a ghost. She stood by my door with the food when her sister Eliza came up, took it from her and threw it at me... I told her that she, her sister and her father all deserved to go to prison and she turned to Martha and said, "You shall catch it for this".'

Although an adjoining neighbour, Mr Wood the baker, had not seen her for the last three years, he had often heard her crying out for bread and water, and groaning all hours of the day and night. He had 'made a stir' in the parish two years ago, but was overruled by the authorities. On more than one occasion his wife had attempted to smuggle rice pudding to Martha, but it was always sent back by her father or sisters.

The Reverend O.W. Davys, rector of Stilton, had discharged his duty by calling a vestry meeting with reference to Crewe and he, along with the churchwardens and other villagers, had gone to him and told him that if he persisted with his cruelty they would proceed against him. Nothing changed and nothing was done about it. Even the local constable John Abbot had turned a blind eye until he heard her screaming for her very life.

Although living close to the family he had not seen the defendant for two years, but was aware that she had been shut up since February 1854 and was continually crying out for food. Matters came to a head when 'I was passing one day and I heard her call out. "Murder!" I demanded to be let in. Her father refused and I then broke the door down. I found one daughter, Rebecca, holding Martha in a small place against the stairs. When I entered Martha held out her hands to me and said, "Oh, help me!"'

He fetched the overseer, Mr Drage, and they took her away despite her sisters trying to prevent them. Martha had to be carried for she was too weak to walk. She was pitifully thin, her body no more than a skeleton. They took her to the Bird in Hand where she was carried upstairs to bed, whimpering that her sisters beat her and her father locked her clothes up. Crewe followed her to the inn and forbade Mr Wright, the local surgeon, to carry out an examination. Eventually permission was obtained, whereupon 'glands' and scrofula were diagnosed. The latter is a tubercular condition commonly known as the 'King's Evil', for by tradition only the touch of a reigning monarch's hand could effect a cure. In his opinion Martha had been very close to death. Wright also told the court that he had last attended her five years ago when he had sent her some cod liver oil, but Crewe returned it and would allow no more contact.

The victim gave her evidence lying on a sofa, still looking more dead than alive. Her sisters were most unkind and used to knock her about. She had tried to leave home on many occasions, but it was impossible, for a constant watch was kept upon her and the doors were always locked. It was nearly five years since she had been let out of the house and her sisters threatened to 'trample her to dust' if she got away. Her father forced her to sleep in his bed so presumably she was sexually abused, but no further details were reported, and her only food was the occasional piece of dry bread.

The three prisoners were then committed for trial at Huntingdon. At the following October Quarter Sessions, Edward, Eliza and Rebecca Crewe were charged with 'unlawfully imprisoning and detaining Martha Crewe from 13th February 1854 to 18th August 1856 and with having assaulted and beaten her, withholding and preventing her from having sufficient food and raiment, with intent to kill and murder her.'

Their victim remained seriously ill. The trial was adjourned until the following March, when the judge, Chief Baron Pollock, sent the father down for three months and his daughters for one month each. The Crewes' sentences were the shortest passed that day, when at the same court the judge ordered 14 years' transportation for a man convicted of setting a straw stack on fire, and a stretch of 8 months in prison for a man convicted of stealing a bushel of potatoes. In his opinion, Martha's tortured young life was of less value than two pieces of cutlery, for he finished his session by penalising a man who had stolen a spoon and a fork to 18 months in Huntingdon Gaol.

UPWARE

The Day They Rescued Cadilly

The original tiny thatched roofed public house called the Five Miles from Anywhere – No Hurry, which stood against the river Cam, was destroyed by fire in the 1950s and replaced by a huge, soulless tourist attraction. This extremely isolated place (hence its name) had no pretensions and was popular with the swashbuckling lightermen who plied the inland waterways in their long strings of cargo barges or lightercraft, which were joined by ropes and long poles. They were exceptionally heavy drinkers, as were the Cambridge undergraduates who made this favoured pub the headquarters of their exclusive club known as the 'Upware Republic', which they ran as a sham country with its own president.

The pub was called the 'Lord Nelson' before being renamed in the 1860s by the eccentric Richard Ramsey Fielder MA, an eccentric graduate of Jesus College and the self styled 'King of Upware' who loved to bait the undergraduates. By whatever name, this sequestered public house was a place for serious drinkers, with maybe the longest ever session starting on the day they rescued Cadilly.

To many, Anna Maria Cadilly was an infamous Cambridge prostitute. To others she was the archetypal 'tart with a heart', good natured and always accessible to her men. They followed her when she holidayed with her sister, whose husband, Millman Smith, looked after a drainage mill at Brandon Creek near Ely. When the weather was pleasant Cadilly took her clients on incredible excursions in her boat *The Willing Maid*, which was moored in Cambridge on the banks of the river Cam against the Little Rose Inn in Trumpington Street.

This good looking woman was born in the early 19th century into a financially secure family from Ely. But young Anna Maria, who enjoyed sex and money, combined the two and earned a good living. After a couple of years whoring around the Fens, Cadilly as she now called herself, put on her best clothes and moved down to Cambridge where she cocked a snook at the law and did a brisk trade, especially with the college set. However, during one freezing winter she was brought to book and thrown into the City lockup to await her punishment, which was to be paraded around the city standing in a cart and dressed only in her shift.

The indignant woman sent word to Millman Smith, begging that he save her from this humiliation which was scheduled for the next day. That evening he rustled up a posse of Fenmen, including one 'Silly Billy' Button, and before daybreak they skated off to save the woman who had pleasured all of them. At that time Silly Billy was unaware of his key role in the escapade. He was a bit simple and had a feminine, peachy smooth face and shrill voice. Although small and mild by nature, when pushed he had the punch of a kangaroo! Uncertain of whether he was male or female, people called him a 'muffmedite', which was their way of saying 'hermaphrodite'. Despite this, young Button was a magnificent speed skater. Not that he ever won a race, for you only had to shout his name and Silly Billy would stop dead, turn round and laugh!

This kindly simpleton loved repeating rhymes and as Cadilly's saviours journeyed down to Cambridge, Millman Smith stayed alongside him muttering over and over,

> 'The students always pay me quick,
> But the townsmen always ask for tick!'

It being market day a large crowd had already gathered around the lockup by the time the rescue party arrived. It took Millman some effort to bribe the beadle to let him visit his sister-in-law, and he managed to smuggle Silly Billy in who, not understanding the implications, swapped clothes with Cadilly. She boldly joined the onlookers to await the outcome.

It was not long before a couple of beefy women were taken in to strip 'Cadilly' down to her shift, but Silly Billy protested in a high voice, refusing to remove his red feathered hat let alone his clothes! One virago held him down whilst the other proceeded to undo his buttons. The indignant prisoner clenched his fists and swearing and cursing like a fish-wife, knocked them senseless. Reinforcements were sent from the Castle gaol, but they too hit the floor.

By now a gang of undergraduates had joined the

102

onlookers who were cheering for Cadilly and yelling, 'Up the gown! Down the town!' for there had always been ill will between the university and the local people. Emotions ran high, a riot was imminent, so with reluctance the authorities had no choice but to bribe Millman Smith to calm the prisoner down and persuade 'her' to take 'her' punishment. It took him half an hour before 'she' climbed into the cart dressed in 'her' undergarments with the millkeeper whispering, 'Tell them the rhyme I told you this morning, Silly Billy. Go on! Tell them the rhyme!'

Happy to oblige he yelled out:

'The students always pay me quick,
But the townsmen always ask for tick!'

This whipped up more hoots and jeers from the students, whilst the townspeople brayed with anger. There was no stopping Silly Billy from shouting the message over and over again in his high pitched voice. Scuffling broke out which swiftly degenerated into a full scale fight. This frightened the patient horse into a gallop, its cart crashing into the stand where the officials stood waiting to denounce Cadilly. The whole lot collapsed in a heap as Silly Billy jumped free and accompanied by his friends and the scarlet woman, skated to the Five Miles from Anywhere – No Hurry.

They did not stop drinking until after the thaw which came a week later, when the grateful Cadilly married Silly Billy and bought a farm at Brandon Creek in Norfolk. A year or two later she gave birth to a strapping boy who eventually took over from his uncle at the mill. However, as we are not told whether or not Cadilly gave up the oldest profession in the world, it remains uncertain if her peachy skinned husband really was a 'muffmedite'.

103

The Headless Queen

A ghostly coach is reputed to thunder down Red Barn Lane on a certain night each year. Drawn by a team of headless horses, inside sits Anne Boleyn, the second of Henry VIII's six wives, who cradles her bloody head in her lap. She is accompanied by her father Sir Thomas Boleyn, the Earl of Wiltshire. It is said they must travel over 40 bridges before daybreak, yet when they reach the river Cam this dreadful apparition takes to the air and flies across the water where there is no bridge.

There is a similar story in neighbouring Norfolk which takes place on the 19th May, the anniversary of the queen's execution, when twelve bridges have to be crossed.

The late J. Wentworth Day, a Fenman and popular author who lived close by, published an article in the December 1964 edition of *Country Life* which included a story set around the shoemaker's shop at neighbouring Wicken. When he was a boy it was called the 'Shimmickey Shop', a place of gossip where the shoemaker, Morley Houghton, read out the news from his daily paper to those who could neither read nor write.

One dark winter's night a frightened poacher rushed into the shop and gasped, 'Oi've jist sin the owd cuch [coach] an' headless hosses in Red Barn Lane. The cuchman set up in it with no hid on his showlders and the back of the cuch is stuck full o' swords and daggers!'

This down to earth soul was scared out of his mind so a group of men got together and, armed with muzzle-loaders and stable forks, made their way to Red Barn Lane by way of a deep ditch. They eventually came across a stationary black coach. A headless steed stood in the shafts, whilst an equally

104

headless man was seated on the box-seat, with swords and the like sticking up in the back. The moon came out at the very moment one of the party fired his gun. The black-headed donkey with a white body brayed its displeasure. The coachman, who happened to be a drunken sweep whose head was snoring against his belly, fell backwards onto his brushes stacked on his cart, where he remained fast asleep as his rig lurched from view steered by the intelligent animal.

This would appear to be the last 'positive sighting' of Anne Boleyn's spectral coach in Red Barn Lane, Upware, but doubtless the story grew in horror as it was told and retold both in this village and in Morley Houghton's 'Shimmickey Shop' at Wicken.

WANSFORD

It Is Definitely In England!

This story of topographical confusion concerns Wansford and its neighbour Stibbington, both mellow stone villages which straddled the former Great North Road before it was re-routed.

The popular Haycock Hotel, which lies close to the river Nene, has a role in the following story. This former posting house, parts of which are believed to date back to the 13th century has a beautiful if puzzling sign bearing the legend, 'What Wansford in England'. It is popularly known as 'The Haycock at Wansford', and is listed in the Peterborough telephone directory and many guide books as being in that village, which the hotel manager confirms to be its correct address. However, the local post office and parish council say this is wrong. The Haycock stands in Stibbington! Yet the mix-up is understandable, for when approaching the building from the north one has to cross the river via the 16th century 'Wansford Bridge' (which is a stone's throw from your destination) and the two villages meet in its middle.

If boundaries can confuse the sober, imagine the bewilderment of someone lying on a makeshift straw sailing craft, spinning round and round in circles whilst recovering from a bout of serious drinking! This is said to have happened in the 16th century, 200 years before 'The Swan' changed its name to The Haycock.

A man from Wansford called Barnaby left this posting house blind drunk. He staggered home across the water meadow, then gave up and clambered on top of a haycock, where presumably he slept for three days and nights, for I am told this is how long it usually takes the floodwaters of the Nene to escape its banks. He did not stir, even when the meadow turned into a lake and his resting place floated away like a piece of flotsam, with him still perched on top slumbering like the innocent. Off he went swirling round and round in the muddy eddies, never stirring until he approached the boundary bridge where a large crowd had gathered.

'Hey you on that haycock! Where do you come from?' someone shouted. The question was repeated a few times as Barnaby's pile of straw miraculously dodged an archway at great speed. Then, awaking with a start and believing he had sailed to some foreign country, the reluctant sailor yelled back, 'I come from Wansford! Wansford in England!' And according to tradition this has been the village's nickname since that day, and the 'Wansford in England' cricket team bears the name with pride.

The story of the drunkard's misadventure is illustrated in wrought iron decorating the hotel's main sign. A much older version hangs over the cooling arch, once used for refreshing the post horses bringing their weary passengers to The Haycock, which to be on the safe side I shall say stands in a beautiful location off the A1 west of Peterborough!

WEST WRATTING

The Spanneys Gate Lady and the Shug Monkey

This parish situated on the Cambridgeshire and Suffolk border is said to have two ghostly apparitions. One is the White Lady, reputed to still haunt the route from Concordia House on the common to Spanneys Gate leading into West Wratting Park. People walking in this vicinity at night occasionally come across her and drivers see her in their headlights, glowing in an 'unearthly light' standing by the road or drifting into the park. Her identity is unknown, but apart from her frightening appearance this is a benign ghost.

Unlike the infamous Shug Monkey, who delighted in scaring people travelling along Slough Hill, a turning off the Balsham road. Within memory few children dared venture here after dark. From this little lane it wandered over to Six Mile Bottom and into West Wickham. There are two versions of this aberration. One likens it to the phantom Black Shuck Dog (see Wicken) with a large black shaggy-coated canine body and big flashing eyes, but unlike the hound with Viking origins, this creature has the face of a monkey. The other saw it as a 7 foot tall monkey with huge eyes as bright as fiery garnets. Either walking on its hind legs or running about on all fours, this amazing creature tormented West Wratting and its neighbours until about the time of the Second World War.

WHITTLESEY WASHES

The Lantern Man

Before being cleared for housing development in the 1950s, there was a large gypsy site at Grays Yard in Bassenhally Road, Whittlesey. Here Eb Smith pitched his horse-drawn wagon when he came down from the Midlands to work on the land. He and his wife Phoebe had five children. Unlike many Romanies Eb did not believe in the supernatural. He dismissed amulets, crystal balls, tea leaves and the fear of the night horrors, and scolded Phoebe for filling the children's head with such notions. As things turned out, she was right after all.

In warm weather the self-igniting marsh gas present in some of the undrained Fen land can produce eerie flickers of light. In Gypsy Smith's time, which is within memory, this natural phenomenon was claimed to be the incarnation of evil creatures with lanterns dangling from their backs. Known collectively as 'Jack o'Lanterns', 'Will o' the Wisps', or 'Jenny Burnt Arses', and singularly as the 'Lantern Man', they were feared by many Fen people and gypsies, who believed they would either kill night wayfarers with their presence, or lure them from safe pathways to drown in the swamps. Parents warned their children that if they saw the 'Lantern Man', their only hope was to lie face down on the ground, hold their breath and hope that he would go away. The evil thing could outrun any human, especially one foolish enough to conjure him up by whistling in the dark!

Eb was a wheeler-dealer who could trill like a bird. One warm summer's night he left Whittlesey to keep an appointment with a man somewhere on Bassen-hally Moor, out on the lonely Whittlesey Washes against the north side of the river Nene. It was the ideal place to do business which called for great privacy. A deal was struck and his accomplice went off in the direction of Thorney, whilst our man walked back towards the Dog in the Doublet bridge and home.

He was pleased. It had been a good haggle with a few pounds in it for himself. He strode out whistling popular tunes, but after a half a mile or so something strange happened. A few hundred yards ahead he noticed a light at ground level. At first no bigger than a speck, it grew larger, then smaller. It jumped up in the air and flew round in circles. It danced on the grass, all the time changing size as if teasing the now decidedly silent onlooker.

You will have to visit these washes alone at night to appreciate the gypsy's apprehension, which soon gave way to full blown fear. Old omens and portents washed through his imagination as the light came speeding towards him. This terrified man ran back deeper into the washland, constantly looking over his shoulder, seeing what could only be the Lantern Man getting closer and closer, now almost as big as himself. Then his mother's words came to mind. There was only one choice! So he lay face down on the grass, held his breath and hoped the bogey man would go away. Fortunately, years of whistling had developed his lungs, so he stayed dead still for a long time, with the little creature jumping up and down, hissing, spitting fire and burning tiny holes in his jacket. Finally it lost interest and Eb was able to return to Bassenhally Road in one piece.

Apparently this experience did not turn him into a law abiding citizen, but it did change his outlook on life. He lost his cynicism, upheld the Romany traditions and learned to read the tea leaves. He even took to wearing an amulet or 'safekeep' hung from a length of string tied around his neck. This was a piece of animal skin upon which someone had written:

ABRACADABRA
BRACADABR
RACADAB
ACADA
CAD
A

which is a traditional and popular local deterrent against all evil.

Some years ago I met an elderly relative of Eb Smith, who confirmed that he often told him this story, which always ended with the unbuttoning of his shirt to reveal the faded lettering. Phoebe predeceased him and, as was the custom, when Eb died his family set fire to his wagon and possessions. Although the talismen went up in flames, his story lives on.

WICKEN

Beware of the Dog!

A gigantic black dog is a common element in folklore in many parts of Great Britain. Throughout East

Anglia it appears as the Galleytrot, Old Snarleyow, Old Scarfe, and most commonly Black Shuck. However, those who cannot bear to speak its name call it the 'Hateful Thing'. Its origins lie with the Viking raiders, for this was the hound of their god Odin, The All-Father.

The creature is still believed to roam this county, for lone walkers out late at night have felt its presence and heard its great chain dragging over the ground. Shuck is about the size of a small calf with eyes which glow either red or yellow, for they can change colour at will. Sometimes they flash, or merge into a huge cyclops eye staring from the centre of his forehead or, even worse, hover over his occasionally headless body! To either see or hear him is reputed to presage either madness or death within the year, yet plenty survive to tell the tale.

This fear was used to good advantage by many coastal smugglers or 'free traders', who would paint a donkey black and hang a red lantern from a harness rigged over its head. There was no better method for keeping superstitious onlookers at bay than to let this 'Hateful Thing' race through their imaginations.

The banks of the river Ouse and much of the Cambridgeshire Fens, including Spinney Bank at Wicken, are his favoured haunts. The following account regarding the latter location is taken from an old typewritten manuscript which does not bear the author's name.

' "He's as big as a calf, wi' eyes that glower at you like bike lamps", local people will assure you. "Do he see you, you'll up and die. That ain't a man living what can see that owd dog and live. Do he goes, he'll goo scatty!"

'A man told a bygone writer that his sister had seen it on her way to meet her sweetheart at a midnight tryst. The spectral dog, "cum along that bank as quiet as death. Jest padded along head down, great owd ears flappin'. That worn't more than 20 yards off when that raised that's head and glouted [glared] at her, its eyes red as blood. My heart! She did holler! She let out a shriek like an owd owl and she belted along that there bank like a hare. Run, sir! There worn't nothin' could ketch her. I reckon if we'd ha' sent her to Newmarket, she'd have won the Town Plate for us! She came bustin' along that bank like a racehorse right slap into her young man. She did holler! And then when he collared hold of her, she went off dead in a faint!"'

This frightful bugbear which crossed the North Sea centuries ago in Viking longboats has become the best known character of this county's folklore. Most local people have either heard of 'Black Shuck' or 'a nasty black dog' and are aware of its power.

WISBECH

The Phantom of the Continental Shoe Repair Shop

In December 1965 the town was not only glowing with Christmas lights but also with ghost fever, for either an alleged one-legged ghost or a poltergeist was causing mayhem in the Continental Shoe Repair shop at 22 High Street. Consequently the general public had need to consider their soles and pay a call in the hope of seeing this phenomenon for themselves.

The first sign of trouble came when a member of staff who was alone in the workroom had his tools snatched from his hands as if by an invisible force.

He told his colleagues, who soon experienced the same thing. Then the lights were switched on and off when there was no one near the switch and doors would burst open with great force. Heavy machinery weighing several tons was moved over-night into different positions. This was surely the work of a ghost? To add to the staff's anxiety, footsteps and the rustle of long skirts were heard on the stairs leading to the empty attic, which for many years had been locked and left empty.

The manager Bill Hyams fetched the key and in the company of a reporter from the *Eastern Daily Press* and the late Ralph Hurst, a freelance photographer, climbed the narrow stairs. He turned the lock and peered into this musty room littered with debris. The trio saw what appeared to be the fresh imprints of a woman's left foot going across the dusty floor from the window to the blocked-up fireplace, avoiding the entrance door. A few days after the story was published, Bill Hyams revisited the 'haunted room' and pulled away the hearth covering. He discovered amongst the soot and bird skeletons, a Victorian scrap book and some women's clothing of that period. Once again a local news reporter was present to record the event. Several years later, Ralph confirmed that it did not appear to be a hoax and he showed me copies of his photos of the 'ghostly' foot marks.

Mr Tony Cornell, then president of the Cambridge University Psychic Research Society, was brought in to investigate the building, but could find no firm evidence of psychic phenomena. However, rumours and speculation were running high. Some 'experts' thought the source of the footprints came from either a one-legged ghost, or a presumably physically-challenged poltergeist who in whatever guise, was responsible for the mischief. The more prosaic dismissed this speculation as poppycock. However, it gave the Continental Shoe Repair shop its proverbial 15 minutes of fame and psychics, sightseers and ghost hunters from all over the country converged upon Wisbech, many bringing crazy theories.

One medium, convinced there was the spirit of a woman in this attic, said all would be well if it were given a rocking chair! Another believed it to be the ghost of Anne Boleyn whom she knew spent every Christmas in Wisbech! If true, this overworked spectre keeps a very low profile. Moreover, what was it doing spending that particular Yuletide hopping about on one leg in the Continental Shoe Repair shop, when it had access to the comforts of the former Boleyn family home at Blickling Hall in Norfolk, in the adjoining county?

When the *Eastern Daily Press* did a re-run of this story on 27th October 1989, Mr Cornell, whom they described as 'probably the best known ghost hunter in the country', was quoted as saying: 'The problem was that the things which were said to be going on were seen by only one person at a time... This part of the town is honeycombed with underground passages, running to the river, and they can have the effect of producing some very strange noises at times. At the same time, that does not explain what a barefooted woman was doing hopping around in an upstairs room.'

The Bride of Mompesson House

The old Horse Fair was developed into a shopping complex in the 1980s, which necessitated the acquisition of the old Salvation Army Citadel. Brand new premises were made available in West Street, on the site of Mompesson House which was demolished for this purpose. Once a fine residence dated 1720, it had degenerated into a shabby apartment block and by the time I moved to the Fens 23 years ago was abandoned to vandals and scrub.

In 1989 I was working on another book and through the local press invited people to share their memories with me. A few weeks later on a vile winter's night, Mr X as I shall call him, stood at my door in the pouring rain, apologising for the intrusion and explaining that he had finally plucked up the courage to cycle twelve miles to tell me something quite amazing if I were interested. Now seriously ill, he reckoned the time had come to share his 30 year old secret.

When he was ten years old he did a newspaper round for Mr Vipan whose shop is still in West Street. It was just before Bonfire Night in 1958 and at about 6.30 in the morning he set off as usual on his deliveries. Mompesson House was his first delivery. He gave the iron gate a hefty push; it was quite a weight for a small boy. He climbed the broken stone steps, opened the unlocked front door and entered the large hallway which always smelled of beeswax polish. Its double staircase led to a gallery landing and the place was still impressive despite its drab flaking decor. There were six tenants whose names, if not their faces, were familiar, for being such an early call the papers were placed on the hall table, where his customers left their money each Friday. It was a perfectly normal November morning on which he experienced something quite wonderful, whilst people slept behind locked doors around and above him.

The last newspaper had been put down when he smelled something different in the air. It was the heady fragrance of lily of the valley, which grew so strong that it masked the smell of the beeswax. Then suddenly a ghostly bride came drifting down the right-hand staircase carrying a posy of the flowers.

115

Her dress was old-fashioned and he could see quite clearly her beautiful face and auburn hair through the lace veil. Mr X was not in the least scared. There was no desire to run away. He was enthralled by the feeling of absolute tranquillity which came with this vision, confiding that it was difficult to explain this emotion without sounding foolish. The spectre stopped at the bottom of the stairs, turned to smile at him, then glided across the hall and up the other staircase before vanishing when she reached the middle of the balcony. Such beauty! Such indescribable peace!

Mr X knows it was his honour to witness that revelation which, even though not overtly religious, brought him the certainty that life does not end with death. He has often drawn upon the wonderful feeling which came with that unearthly woman. He spoke with such sincerity and had ridden his bike such a long way through terrible weather that I did not doubt his honesty. He finished by saying that when the demolition team came to raze the building to the ground, he watched them tearfully from across the road until their work was done.

Since then others have told me of seeing a 'White Lady' in that Georgian house, but none experienced the marvellous bridal vision. When I pass the Citadel I often think of that gentle person standing on the dusty pavement watching the men with their remorseless ball and chain. I too can imagine the peaceful vision carrying white perfumed flowers and its positive effect on that young newspaper boy.

YAXLEY

Look Before You Sleep

When body-snatchers were making a living from the dead in the early part of the 19th century, there was a local man who spent most of his spare time fishing and visiting alehouses. After a bout of solid drinking it was of little consequence where he slept. In a ditch, behind a hedge, in a field or even in the middle of the road, he was in no position to be selective. His tolerant wife was used to an empty bed, so remained unconcerned when he was absent on one particularly memorable occasion.

After a day by the river he had every intention of going home, but with his belly awash with beer and his head spinning round in circles, knew it was useless to try. In the middle of nowhere he came upon a barn, kicked the door open and collapsed onto a sack of something which, although a bit bumpy and a trifle smelly, was good enough for him. After a good night's sleep he set about investigating the contents of his uncomfortable resting place. The string around its neck was fastened very securely, but he picked away at the knots and eventually pulled out the body of a young woman.

Now one of the finest aids to sobriety is to discover that you have spent a few hours slumbering on top of a corpse. After much explaining, the poor chap learned at the following Coroner's Inquest that his makeshift mattress had been 24 year old Elizabeth Fry, late of Peterborough cemetery. Her body had been disinterred by grave robbers working for the very surgeon who owned the barn in which he had dossed. However, being a man of high standing within the local community the incident was hushed up and no charges made. Presumably the Yaxley man vowed to drink less and to make sure that the next time he fell asleep on a woman, he would first check to make sure she was breathing!

THE DEAD ON THE MOVE

Resurrectionists, better known as body-snatchers, were particularly busy from the latter half of the 18th century until the passing of the Anatomy Act of 1832. These men made a living from stealing corpses from recently buried coffins to supply the requirements of medical schools and individuals. The medical profession and defence lawyers justified the crime on the grounds that this science could not be advanced without the dissection of cadavers. Dead people had no further use of their bodies which could benefit the living. The robbers always took the deceased naked, which in law was classified a misdemeanour. To remove a body clothed was a felony and carried a far harsher punishment.

Mike Petty, Principal Librarian of the Local Studies section of the county library, took part in a programme called *Ghostly Echoes* broadcast on BBC Radio Cambridgeshire on 16th April 1995. This comprised a number of stories mainly trawled from old press reports held in his archives. He said that during the 1820s the dead were certainly on the move in this county – and they had help.

On 27th November 1827 the body of John Golding, recently deceased, was disinterred from **Cherry Hinton** churchyard near Cambridge. The grave was examined in the presence of the vicar, curate and churchwardens, and showed the casket had been forced open and the body removed. All that remained were the shroud and the clothes attached to the corpse which were rolled together and left inside the coffin.

Then 15th February 1828 brought news of a hamper having been taken to the Horse and Gate Inn, **Chatteris** in the north of the county and booked by the

119

Wisbech coach to London. On arrival the string securing the lid had broken loose and inside were the remains of a female and two infants. There was much fear amongst those who had lately buried their loved ones. One grave of a recently deceased child was opened by the parents. The corpse had gone. Just its burial clothes remained, neatly folded.

At **Doddington** near March, the body of a female was interred and the neighbours set up a watch. A little after midnight two men crept towards the grave and commenced their gruesome work, but the alarm was given too quickly and they escaped without trace.

On 7th November of that year, resurrectionists were at work in **Stanground** near Peterborough. They had snatched the body of a man recently buried in the churchyard. A suspect was questioned by the authorities, but his companions had fled, leaving their tools in a ditch and their horse and cart at Norman Cross.

These dreadful incidents, and there are plenty more, must have placed a terrible strain not only on the recently bereaved, but also on the sick and vulnerable. Many sad people were compelled to keep watch over mounds of bare earth, waiting for their loved ones to decay and therefore rest in peace.

BIBLIOGRAPHY

Railway World, Vol. 36. No. 418. February 1975

D.I. Gordon, *A Regional History of the Railways of Great Britain*, Vol. 5 – Eastern Counties, David & Charles, Newton Abbot (1968)

W.H. Barrett, *Tales from the Fens*, Routledge & Kegan Paul (1964)

W.H. Barrett, *More tales from the Fens*, Routledge & Kegan Paul (1966)

Edith Porter, *Cambridgeshire Customs and Folklore*, Routledge & Kegan Paul (1969)

Cambridgeshire, Huntingdon and Peterborough Life April 1969

Joan Forman, *Haunted East Anglia*, Jarrold Colour Publications, Norwich (1974)

Geoff Yeates, *Cambridge College Ghosts*, Jarrold Publishing, Norwich (1994)

Cambridgeshire Federation of Women's Institutes, *The Cambridgeshire Village Book*, Countryside Books (1989)

W.H.B. Saunders, *Legends & Traditions of Huntingdonshire*, Simpkin Marshall & Co (1913)

Mini Stories from the Fens, Compiled and published by Trevor Bevis, March, Cambs

Fenland Places Revisited, written and published by Trevor Bevis, March, Cambs

Christopher Marlow, *Legends of the Fenland People*, Cecil Palmer (1926)

C.F. Tebbut, *St. Neots*, Phillimore (1984)

Folklore of the British Isles, Chosen by Kevin Crossley-Holland, The Folio Society (1985)

Trevor Hickman, *The History of Stilton Cheese*, Alan Sutton Publishing Ltd

Lucy M. Boston, *The Children of Green Knowe*, Puffin Books (1975)

121

OTHER SOURCES

Ghostly Echos recorded by Mike Petty for BBC Radio Cambridgeshire 1995

ACKNOWLEDGEMENTS

I thank all who have given their help. Please accept my apologies if any names have been omitted from the following list: Mike Petty, Principal Librarian Local Studies, Cambridgeshire County Library; Trevor Bevis; Diana Boston; Michael Moore; Paul Henderson; Ely Tourist Information Centre; Barrie Hakes; John Raines; Paul Orridge; Jan Hemming-Allen; Ralph Hurst (deceased); John Bradshaw; Levi Smith; David Ebbs; Liam McGivern and the staff of the Bell Inn, Stilton; Vera Cowlan; members of various Women's Institutes, Over Sixties clubs and other community groups.

INDEX